Best of Breed

THE **SHIH TZU**

Your Essential Guide
From Puppy To
Senior Dog

Edited By

**Juliette
Cunliffe**

ACKNOWLEDGEMENTS

The publishers would like to thank the following for help with photography: Margaret Stangeland (Weatsom); Tracey Hitt (Miracey); Carol Stubbs (Sonoma); Gill Ace (Matsonic); Pat Lord (Huxlor); Carol Ann Johnson; Hearing Dogs for Deaf People; Pets As Therapy. Special thanks are due to Juliette Cunliffe for use of images from her extensive personal collection.

Cover photo: © Tracy Morgan Animal Photography (www.animalphotographer.co.uk)
Dog featured is Ethelsmead Dirty Dancing owned by Mrs J. Rutter.

Pages 2 and 63© istockphoto.com/Ken Hurst; page 12 © istockphoto.com/Wilson Valentin;
Page 53 © istockphoto.com/Steve Pepple; page 65 © istockphoto.com/Jerry Schiller;
Page 135 © istockphoto.com/Eric Isselée.

The British Breed Standard reproduced in Chapter 7 is the copyright of the Kennel Club and published with the club's kind permission. Extracts from the American Breed Standard are reproduced by kind permission of the American Kennel Club.

THE QUESTION OF GENDER
**The 'he' pronoun is used throughout this book instead of the rather impersonal 'it',
but no gender bias is intended**

First published in 2010 by the Pet Book Publishing Company Limited
St Martin's Farm, Chapel Lane, Zeals, Wiltshire BA12 6NZ

Reprinted in 2012

This edition first published in 2015

© 2015 Pet Book Publishing Company Limited.
Printed and bound in South Korea.

ISBN
978-1-910488-05-8
1-910488-05-4

CONTENTS

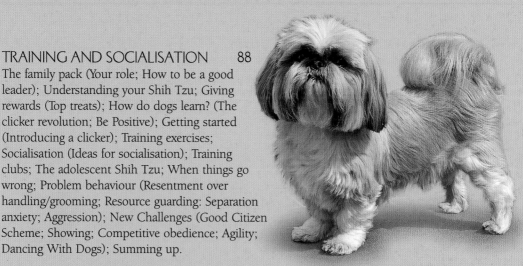

GETTING TO KNOW THE SHIH TZU

Chapter 1

The Shih Tzu is a truly charming little character, full of fun and with the sweetest personality; small and yet not so small as some – indeed he is rather sturdy in his frame. His long, flowing coat, chrysanthemum-like face and attractive 'top knot' that shows off his oriental expression, require a lot of work, but the finished result is well worth the effort. Many Shih Tzu kept as pets rather than for the show ring are kept in short coat, often known as 'puppy trim', but still they look enchanting.

A TYPICAL SHIH TZU

The Shih Tzu is unrivalled as a companion dog and the breed was much loved in China and also in the West. Now its popularity has spread across the globe and there are many enthusiastic supporters of the breed in numerous countries. In many of these it ranks among the numerically highest, both among showgoers and pet owners. Sometimes owners of Shih Tzu travel for miles to show their dogs, frequently from one continent to another. When I have judged this breed abroad, I have been heartened by the enthusiasm of breeders and exhibitors whose thirst for knowledge knows no bounds, especially in countries where the show scene is less well developed than it is in Britain and the USA.

I have occasionally met devastated exhibitors who have arrived too late for competition after travelling hundreds of miles from another country. This has resulted in me only being able to give a general appraisal of the dog, without judging it, but these stalwart, dedicated owners have taken it all in their stride, and, at the end of the day, have turned tail and set off again in a homeward direction, seemingly just glad to have received my opinion.

BREED ORIGINS

The Shih Tzu has its roots in Tibet, where one of its close relatives is the Lhasa Apso, a truly Tibetan breed with a much stronger character than its Sino-Tibetan cousin. For several centuries Lhasa Apsos were taken to China, often as gifts to high dignitaries and also to be given as tribute gifts en route to ensure safe passage in what was then a very difficult and often dangerous land. In China the Lhasa Apso and Pekingese were bred together and so the Shih Tzu was created.

There are other theories as to the origin of the ShihTzu, one being that three temple dogs were taken to China in about 1650 and that from these three dogs the Shih Tzu was

7

developed. We shall read more about the history of the Shih Tzu and this alternative theory in the next chapter. However, I am among the majority who believe that the true history of the breed lies in the Apso-Pekingese cross, and knowing this from the outset, it is easy to see why the breed is the shape it is.

BREED CHARACTERISTICS

The Shih Tzu is technically half an inch taller than the Lhasa Apso, according to the UK Breed Standard, but "lower slung", with a more barrelled rib shape and more bow in the forelegs to accommodate the ribbing. The foreface is certainly not so short as that of the Pekingese, and yet shorter than that of the Lhasa Apso. The skull shape is more round than that of the Lhasa Apso, so the hair needs to be tied up in a top-knot, or it truly would fall all over the eyes. The Lhasa Apso's skull is narrower so the hair only forms a veil and therefore the Apso can see perfectly well, even with his hair loose.

Like his ancestors, the Shih Tzu has a gloriously long, double coat that cascades to the ground. It does not shed but just grows and grows, which also means that the undercoat forms mats and knots if it is not groomed

When you see a Shih Tzu (left) and a Lhasa Apso (right) in pet trim, you can pinpoint the differences between the two breeds more easily.

thoroughly on a regular basis. Historically, people have always considered that the Shih Tzu is an untrimmed breed, as it should never by sculpted by scissoring. However, it is generally accepted that a little discreet 'tidying up' is necessary at floor length, and under the feet where knots can so easily form between the pads if the hair is not carefully removed. Having said that, the well-padded feet should appear big, on account of the wealth of hair, so under no circumstances should trimming be taken to the extreme.

The non-shedding nature of the coat makes this a breed

worthy of serious consideration by dog lovers who are allergy sufferers, but careful exposure trials should be carried out before coming to a conclusive decision.

Common to both the Lhasa Apso and the Pekingese, the Shih Tzu carries his tail over his back, lifted rather higher than on his Tibetan cousin. With his distinctive head, tail and coat, when moving the Shih Tzu is often described as being "like a ship in full sail". No wonder this little breed with his tremendous character has so many admirers!

All coat colours are acceptable, adding to the visual pleasure of the breed. Colours range through various shades of gold to red and greys through to black. In this breed, liver and chocolate are also acceptable, which means the nose pigment in these colours is correspondingly a dark liver, while in other colours it is black. Colours may be solid or parti-coloured, and in the latter case a white blaze on the forehead and white tip to the tail are highly prized features.

The Breed Standard will be analysed in depth later (see Chapter Seven), but it is important at this stage to know

SHIH TZU COLOURS

Gold and white.

Red and white.

Brindle and white.

Black and white.

that the Shih Tzu has a wide mouth that is generally slightly undershot, or it may be level. The Breed Standard also states that the lips should be level so this, in effect, places a restriction on how far undershot the mouth may be. If it was overly undershot, the lips would not meet and this would entirely spoil the Shih Tzu's charming, oriental expression.

In the next chapter we shall read about some of the gloriously quaint Chinese descriptions of the breed's physical attributes, but while we are on the subject of the Shih Tzu's mouth, 'water caltrop mouth', 'frog mouth' and 'charcoal heater mouth' will serve as just a 'taster' for the moment.

As for all dogs, but especially the shorter-faced breeds whose teeth are packed fairly tightly together, tooth care is an essential part of canine maintenance. Even from an early age, owners should get their Shih Tzu used to having their teeth cleaned regularly to prevent the occurrence of dental problems and gum disease.

THE SHIH TZU AS A COMPANION DOG

The Shih Tzu was not bred as a guardian, nor to work, but purely as a much-loved and highly prized pet. Shih Tzu love human

The Shih Tzu thrives on human companionship.

companionship, and usually get along well with other dogs, too. This is not an antagonistic breed; a Shih Tzu tends to take everything in his stride so fits in well with the majority of household situations. Like all dogs, the Shih Tzu does bark – but only with reason – and the barking is not usually excessive.

Although Shih Tzu adore their owners, they are not always as obedient as might be hoped, for they have a bit of a stubborn streak. A Shih Tzu likes to think things out for himself, for he is highly intelligent and sees no point in doing anything without good reason. The breed's outgoing personality makes the Shih Tzu a joy to live with; sometimes he likes to be in the very middle of things, while at

other times he can appear somewhat 'above' whatever is going on around him. He can be full of fun and his clownish antics can be amusing to watch. How unfair it would be to deprive a Shih Tzu of a happy family environment and to restrict him purely to life as a kennel dog. This is a breed whose ancestors were used to being pampered in Peking's Royal Palace, and they certainly believe they are destined to live in more luxurious surroundings than those of a simple kennel!

Many Shih Tzu love to play with balls and toys, and it is a joy to watch your pet running around, not always able to pick up the ball, but chasing it hither and thither to his heart's content. At other times, a Shih Tzu can be perfectly tranquil and still, but then, seemingly without thought or reason, he decides to dash around at a great rate of knots and play the fool. It makes you wonder just what goes on inside your Shih Tzu's head; those tranquil moments are probably spent planning the next game.

Another endearing habit that is common to a good many Shih Tzu is 'begging'. A Shih Tzu does not merely give a paw but sits upright, bottom to the ground, and front legs hanging down; a cute, little face invariably looking up at his owner, or whoever has taken his fancy – probably the person in the room with the largest slice of cake! When greeting special friends, the Shih Tzu has a sweet habit of bobbing about on his hind legs, with front paws waving about in front of his head.

The Shih Tzu also 'talks', usually when greeting people or trying to get someone's attention. This is a kind of soft, chortling sound, emanating from the back of the throat, and those unacquainted with the Shih Tzu occasionally mistake it for growling. This is certainly not the case, but, like any dog, the Shih Tzu can, understandably, be a bit grouchy if treated roughly.

This is a breed that is deserving of love and attention; they thrive on it. Eminent breeder Dorothy Gurney said she had one Shih Tzu bitch who actually cried when she was left alone, showing a pathetic, crumpled, tear-stained face. This little bitch was obviously the exception to the rule but, nonetheless, a Shih Tzu is not happy if he is not involved with you in your family life. Even if you decided to keep more than one Shih Tzu, this should not present a problem. Most owners find that several can live happily together without a cross word between them, though a few males can be rather dominant.

PET OR SHOW
Hopefully if you decide the Shih Tzu is the right choice of dog for you and your family, you will have done so for many good reasons, not just the breed's glamour. There is no doubting that this is a highly striking and attractive breed, but beauty is only skin deep and the Shih Tzu's personality must appeal to you, too.

It is, of course, possible to combine the best of both worlds: to have a dog as a show dog and as a pet. The long coat, though, takes a great deal of care and preparation, especially for the show ring. For this reason, many owners tend to clip a dog down as he gets older and copes less easily with the laborious task of being bathed, groomed and dried. Many owners of show dogs clip them off immediately they retire them from the ring, and this is quite understandable too, just so long as the coat, be it long or short, is kept in tip-top condition.

There is no more endearing sight than a Shih Tzu in classic 'begging' position.

If a Shih Tzu is kept purely as a pet, many owners clip down the coat, or have the coat clipped by a professional dog groomer three or four times a year. This costs money each time, but is nowhere near the expense of purchasing the many grooming products that are necessary to retain a Shih Tzu's glorious show coat. When kept in short coat, Shih Tzu can join in every type of activity their owners wish, without worrying too much about an enormous amount of work afterwards. However, any pieces of debris that have become attached to the coat will need to be removed immediately upon returning

home, whether the coat be long or short. It is also extremely important to check feet and between the pads to be sure nothing has become trapped, and a quick ear inspection is also advisable in case a grass seed has worked its way inside.

If owners are dedicated, long-coated Shih Tzu can also enjoy plenty of fun. Show dogs love romps in the countryside, too, but their owners have to be prepared to put in the work on returning home.

SHIH TZU AND CHILDREN
Most Shih Tzu get along well with children for this is a very

accommodating breed. However, children's parents and guardians must be aware that a small child can all too easily hurt a Shih Tzu by pulling at his tempting, long, flowing locks. This can be painful for any long-coated breed and although most Shih Tzu will tolerate a lot, a painful tug at the coat might just, understandably, be too much.

Another temptation for tiny tots is to poke fingers into the Shih Tzu's attractive round eyes; again this is an absolute 'no no'. Children can also be noisy, and not all Shih Tzu appreciate this, though some don't seem to mind at all.

As with all children and dog relationships, parental guidance and control plays a vital role, and sensible introductions and upbringing can mean the difference between harmony and discontent in a household.

SHIH TZU AND OTHER PETS
Because of the Shih Tzu's tolerant temperament, the breed usually gets along well with other dogs and, in many cases, with other household pets. When a number of Shih Tzu are kept together, they often become the firmest of friends. This is also the case when they have the companionship of other breeds, even if those dogs are larger than themselves. However, if the other breed is particularly fiery or antagonistic, a Shih Tzu may not stand it. He is a

A Shih Tzu will probably be happier living with older children.

Shih Tzu are very sociable and enjoy being kept as a mini-pack.

laidback sort of character and it would be a pity to change this by forcing him to live with another animal that puts him always on the defence – and he is certainly capable of defending himself when his hackles get raised.

So if you already have other dogs in your family, take a careful look at their temperaments before deciding that the Shih Tzu is the right breed to join them. Even a Shih Tzu who considers himself 'top dog' is rarely aggressive and he should not be put into a situation where he feels the need to be.

I would always caution owners of any breed of dog to take particular care with small family pets, such as mice, rats, hamsters and guinea pigs; even rabbits might get into trouble, with a small dog as well as larger one. Having said that, the tolerant Shih Tzu might well become friends with small pets, too. My own pets have formed some very unusual bonds. I once had a Hill

Mynah Bird who got along very well with our large, white family cat, and I had a Rough Collie who, when dusk was falling, always rounded up the miniature rabbit who ran free around the garden. In the case of the Shih Tzu, as indeed with any breed, it is careful and sensible introduction to one another that is important, for this will set the road for a happy bond of friendship.

As with most breeds, owners should always exercise caution around the time of a bitch's heat, both for a little while before, during, and for a couple of weeks afterwards. At this time bitches who are usually the best of friends can be a little touchy with one another, and, of course, males and females must certainly be kept apart while a season is in progress. At this time, if you keep more than one male, you may also find that the males are more competitive with each other. But this is normal canine behaviour

and, in general, the Shih Tzu is relatively easy to manage in this respect.

EXERCISE
The Shih Tzu does not actually need an enormous amount of exercise but, nonetheless, he will always appreciate a good walk so that he can investigate new sights and smells to stimulate his senses. Being the friendly chap he is, he will enjoy meeting friends and acquaintances along the way, be they human or canine, and you can be very proud of his sociable behaviour.

However, if your Shih Tzu is kept in long coat, you will have to pay special attention to where he is exercised, as his flowing robes will pick up every ounce of dirt and debris, so will need to be carefully tended to upon return home after his walk. Obviously he will need an exercise area at home, so a garden is important to him, though it need not necessarily be large. Even a large patio can be suitable if he is also taken out for walks.

If two or more Shih Tzu are kept together and have developed a friendship, they will spend many a happy hour exercising each other. They will love to romp and play together and in doing so will use up considerably more energy than they would if they lived alone.

Owners who keep their pet Shih Tzu in short coat can allow their canine companions considerably more freedom regarding where they are exercised, but even a short coat can get wet and dirty, so will still need checking over thoroughly at the end of each walk.

HEALTH AND LIFE SPAN

The Shih Tzu is a long-lived breed. It is not at all unusual for a Shih Tzu to reach 14, 15 or even 16 years of age, and the occasional Shih Tzu lives even longer than this. Bearing this in mind, when you take on a Shih Tzu puppy, you must be prepared to be his true companion for many a long year ahead.

Like all breeds of dog, and mongrels and crossbreeds too, there are certain health issues connected with the breed and, of course, a dog with a serious health problem may indeed have a shorter life span. More information relating to the health of the Shih Tzu will be found in Chapter 8.

ASSISTANCE DOGS

The Shih Tzu was bred to be an outstanding companion, and this means he can be highly valued in the role of assistance dog, as he bonds so closely with people.

THERAPY DOGS

The Shih Tzu makes a wonderful therapy dog, as his appearance, size and personality make him popular with almost everyone. When well trained, a Shih Tzu can be taken along to homes to visit the elderly or infirm, and these visits are greatly looked forward to. The Shih Tzu's small size and yet sturdy build makes him very suitable to be petted and to sit on people's laps should he be allowed to do so. It is great to know that your own canine friend is giving pleasure to someone else who needs animal companionship but is unable, due to personal circumstances, to have this on a permanent basis.

HEARING DOGS

The Shih Tzu is an alert, attentive little dog, which makes him a

A Shih Tzu in full coat will love the chance to explore – but you will have to give him a good tidy-up when he returns home.

Small in size, and friendly in disposition, the Shih Tzu is an ideal therapy dog.

The quick-witted Shih Tzu is highly valued as a Hearing dog.

This is Amber waiting by the phone to ring. As soon as it rings, she will alert her master.
Photo: Darren Cooper, NEC, Birmingham, UK.

good contender as a hearing dog for the deaf. He can be trained to alert his owner to sounds such as the doorbell or telephone ringing, the alarm clock or even fire alarms. A well-trained hearing dog can make all the difference in the world to someone with impaired hearing.

SUMMING UP

Taking everything into consideration, if you are prepared to dedicate time to the Shih Tzu's coat, the chances are that if you have read this far and are still interested in owning the breed, the Shih Tzu may just be the right dog for you. But

remember that if you are part of a family, this important decision must be taken by everyone who will be involved in your pet's future life, so sit down together and discuss every aspect of what will lie ahead if you decide that a Shih Tzu will join you in your home.

15

THE FIRST SHIH TZU

Chapter 2

Let me begin by clarifying that Shih Tzu is both singular and plural, so here we are not endeavouring to find the first ever specimen of a Shih Tzu, which would be impossible, but using Shih Tzu in its collective term to delve into the history of the breed in general.

Buddhism had spread from India into Tibet during the seventh century, but it was not until the time of Kublai Khan, in 1253, that this religion was adopted in China. In Buddhism the lion played an important role; not that this was an animal indigenous to China, but it had been imported there as a gift for Emperors from as early as AD87. Early artists, though, were not familiar with the real animal, which led to the lion being depicted in many different ways over the centuries.

Buddha Manjusri, the god of learning, was believed to travel round dressed as a simple priest, but with him was a small Chinese Ha-pa dog that could be

transformed into a lion so that the Buddha could ride on his back. China's Manchu Emperors, who where regarded as the Sun and Sons of Heaven, held the

Pictured left is Wenshu (Manjusri) Buddha riding on a lion, with other deities riding an elephant and a hou (Fung Shen Pang).

Buddha's small dog-lion or lion-dog in the highest regard, for they, too, were considered by their flatterers as symbols of the Buddha. The Chinese authorities claimed that the name 'Manchu' was actually based on the Tibetan name 'Manjusri'.

However, it is the mythological Snow Lion that is considered the king of animals, and it is the Snow Lion with which the Shih Tzu and its cousin, the Lhasa Apso, are most closely connected. This white lion is so powerful that when he roars, seven dragons fall out of the sky! He can leap and turn in an instant, and can walk in both mist and cloud. His voice is that of the Middle Way, of truth and fearlessness, which can subdue all. How privileged are these breeds to be connected with such a marvellous beast!

I mentioned earlier that Tibet is considered the ancestral home of the Shih Tzu because one of its ancestors is the Lhasa Apso. This breed was used as a tribute gift to ensure safe passage when

travelling from Tibet into China, a journey that could take eight to ten months. The Lhasa Apso is not, and never has been, a sacred dog, but has always been held in high esteem; it is frequently believed to be the reincarnation of a monk who has erred in a previous life.

I state that it was the Lhasa Apso that was used as a tribute gift for safe passage, and that is true, but we should also bear in mind that the Tibetans used not to be clear about the naming of their breeds, so crossings did take place on occasion and other breeds might also have been involved to a lesser extent. This is evidenced by the fact that sometimes when two pure-bred Shih Tzu, or indeed two pure-bred Lhasa Apsos, are mated together they can produce what, to all intents and purposes, looks like a Tibetan Spaniel.

There is no doubt that small, hairy dogs found themselves in China, though their birthplace had been Tibet. There they were crossed with other small dogs,

which were already in that vast country, China.

THE SMALL DOGS OF CHINA

Around 1760BC Emperor Tang accepted 'square dogs' as tribute gifts, but no size appears to have been recorded, and the very fact that they are square makes it more likely that they were more closely connected to the Chow Chow than today's smaller Chinese breeds. Around the time of Confucious in about 500BC, it was recorded that when going to the chase, a favourite pastime of the Chinese, one kind of dog followed his master's chariot and others, with short mouths, were carried in the carts. This leads us to believe that those with 'short mouths' were fairly small, so here may lie a connection with today's Shih Tzu.

It has been said that when puppies were between three and seven days old, the nose cartilage was crushed with a thumb-nail or a chopstick to make them shorter. But this may well not have been true, at least not for all, for the British Museum houses the skull of an early short-nosed dog, and in this the bones of the nose were naturally short.

We know that by the end of the first century AD, the Emperors had begun to take an interest in small dogs and in 'Pai' dogs, which were short-legged dogs that belonged under the table. We should keep in mind that tables were very low, so the dogs were certainly small. Small dogs were held in high regard at

Lions in lacquered wood, Peking.

Chinese Lo-Sze or Pug dog, Peking 1914.

Lo–Sze Dog.

that time and many had honours bestowed on them. In AD168, Emperor Ling Ti kept one in his garden and he was so fond of it that he awarded it the Chow-Hsien grade, the highest literary rank of the period. Giving titles to small dogs was not at all unusual, and highly ranked dogs were often given soldiers to guard them. They were fed on only the very best rice and meat, and had the choicest carpets on which to sleep. It seems that being a small dog in China in those days was not an unpleasant life at all; how very sad it is that things changed so in future times.

Small dogs arrived in China from Russia, Persia (now Iran) and Turkey, the silk trade between the Eastern Roman or Byzantine Empire and China being of considerable importance both to China and to the West. Two remarkable small dogs, a male and a female, came from Fu Lin in AD624; this may have been the Chinese transliteration of the origin of the name of Istanbul. They measured 19 cms high (7.5 ins) and 32 cms (12.5 ins) long and even as late as the 17th century, descendents of these dogs were still known as Fu Lin. One of their colloquial names, though, was 'ha-pa', which, when translated, means 'pet' or 'lap' dog with short legs. So here again we have the Ha-pa Dog. This little dog was also known by the name of 'Shih Tzu Kou' or 'lion dog', so we appear to have evidence that some of these 'under the table dogs' had long coats, very probably making them distant ancestors of the Shih Tzu we know today.

These little dogs were reputed for their remarkable intelligence; they knew how to carry a torch in their mouths and could even drag a horse by its bridle. It is possible that their ancestry went back to the Maltese-type dog for some of these dogs went to Turkey from Malta.

MONKEY-LION DOG AND HAND DOGS

In Shantung Province, we find small dogs called not only Ha-pa but also 'Turkish dogs', 'pugs' or 'Lo-sze'. Some were short-haired, but others had long coats and were referred to as 'monkey-lion dogs'; locally they were called 'Shih nung kou', meaning fierce, shaggy-haired watch dog.

The term 'monkey-lion dog' came about from a charming legend. A lion met a small monkey in a forest and fell in love with her, but their great difference in size made their union impossible. So the lion prayed to the Buddha to make him small enough to find favour with the monkey, while at the same time pleading that his great heart would remain intact so he was no less in love than before. In his compassion, the Lord Buddha turned him into a Lion Dog, changing his stature, but not his mighty heart.

Another rather quaint name came about for the 'pug dogs', which were introduced as far as Lhasa where they were known as 'Lags K'ye' meaning 'hand dog'. This was because if a human were to lay hands on a freshly hatched young eagle, the bird would be transformed into a Chinese pug dog. Between AD990 and 994 the 'Lo-chiang dog', another form of pug, was sent to the Emperor from Ssuch'uan Province. These dogs were very intelligent, tame and docile; they sat beside the Emperor, wagging their tails and barking.

Golden-coated, nimble dogs were commonly bred by people in their homes in China in AD1300, and these were described as resembling the lion. The Emperor of the time was said to have loved dogs so much that he stole them from his subjects.

THE NINETEENTH CENTURY

By 1820 the cult of the lap dog reigned supreme in China. Very tiny dogs, later known as 'sleeve dogs', were the very height of fashion and unfortunately dogs were stunted by artificial means so that they might be raised as dwarf dogs.

Various methods were used to stunt their growth, one of which was to restrict their exercise from the third month to maturity in an endeavour to reduce food intake and therefore retard growth. Another method was to hold a young, growing puppy in the hand for days at a time; by using gentle pressure of the fingers a slight exaggeration of width between the shoulders was achieved.

Yet another strange method used was to feed the puppy with sugar, but it was thought that the fact that this caused the puppy to drink more caused the nose to lengthen, especially during the third month when nose development was at its greatest. The most intense growth of the legs was reckoned to be during the fourth month; to arrest

development, only strong soup but no water was given to the puppies. A particularly cruel method was to raise the puppies in wire cages that closely fitted the body; these were not removed until maturity was reached.

Other than the possible crushing of cartilage to keep noses short, some puppies were fed from a flat plate, or, from three months onwards, were encouraged to bite on a pig-skin, stretched on a board. Others had their noses massaged every day.

SLAUGHTER OF DOGS

It is widely known that dog meat is eaten in China, but it is not only larger dogs like the Chow Chow that have suffered at the hands of the Chinese. There were numerous dog farms, especially in Manchuria, and, in many of these, smaller dogs were raised and slaughtered for their coats.

When a girl was married she was often given about six dogs as her dowry. From these she could breed a good number of puppies each year, so her fortune grew rapidly. Timing was of the essence, for the coat was at its best during the winter. Bearing in mind that the puppies' coats had matured sufficiently by the age of six to eight months, the dogs were destroyed before the thaw set in. The poor dogs were killed by strangulation so as not to damage the pelt. The skins were then dried and frozen until they reached market where they were cured before the thaw affected them. They were made into mats

From a scroll of 100 Pekingese.

and robes, and, even as late as the 1930s, large numbers found their way to European markets, for they closely resembled wolf and fox furs.

THE DOWAGER EMPRESS TZU HSI

The Dowager Empress Tzu Hsi, born in 1835, began her life in the Imperial Palace as a concubine and ended up ruling China. The Emperor's primary wife had no sons and so it was that when he died, Tzu Hsi's five-year-old son became Emperor. Although she could not rule the country openly, a bamboo screen was erected behind the boy's throne so that she could listen to the officials' reports and tell her son how to reply.

Tzu Hsi's son died as a young man following smallpox, though his actual death may have been due to venereal disease. His wife committed suicide and so the Dowager Empress chose her own three-year-old nephew to inherit the throne. That's how much of an influential lady she was!

But interesting as her life may have been, it is her love of dogs upon which we shall concentrate here. She was an infamous, over-indulgent dog lover who owned Pekingese, Pugs and Shih Tzu. In 1903, Katherine Carl was a guest of the Imperial Court for 10 months and, through her, we have been able to learn much about the way the palace dogs were treated.

It is believed that among the hundreds of dogs in the palace,

Taken from the Imperial Scroll, painted in 1890 by Miao Su-Chiun, instructress in painting to the Dowager Empress.
Pictured (left) is the long-coated Hah-Pah Dog, 'Li-Erh', meaning 'Pear', who was sent from Tibet as a gift to the Emperor. The dog's temperament was said to be like that of a 'human being'. The length of body was given as 1ft 5ins (42cms), and the height is 8ins (20cms).

the Shih Tzu were regarded as the Imperial family's personal property, so were rarely seen outside the palace walls. Although mainly golds and gold and white parti-colours seemed to predominate, she certainly had at least one black dog, too, probably several. Being an artist, she was chiefly interested in breeding for colour and to develop symmetrical markings.

Thankfully, the Empress strongly disagreed with the development of abnormalities, and tried hard to avoid bowed legs and protruding tongues. Although there are reports of her not having agreed with the more drastic measures of keeping noses short, she did reportedly stroke and massage dogs' noses and

made them chew on stretched leather in her personal endeavours to keep them short. In doing so she produced the much-desired flatness of face in her Pekingese. Interestingly, in Collier's Dogs of China and Japan in Nature and in Art, he notes that one of the Empress's favourite dogs was of the long-coated variety, which she called Tibetan. He goes on to say, though, that she was not successful in breeding this delicate race.

In 1908, His Holiness The Dalai Lama presented several dogs to the Dowager Empress. Several foreigners saw these dogs, called 'Shih Tzu Kou'. Considering them a treasured gift, she kept them apart from her

Pekingese Dog by Tsou Yi-Kwei (1686-1766).

Chinese Pug. From an Imperial dog book by Tsou-Yi-Kwei (1686-1766).

Lion Dog from an Imperial dog book.

Pekingese, in order to keep them distinct and to maintain their breed characteristics. Presumably these were the 'Tibetans' referred to above. As luck would have it, the 'Shih Tzu Kou' arrived only shortly before her death on 15 November of that same year, at the age of 73.

Although the palace eunuchs continued to breed the dogs, it is highly likely that experimental crosses took place, causing a divergence of type. It is generally believed that the eunuchs bred three short-nosed breeds inside the palace: the Pug, the Pekingese, and the breed we know today as the Shih Tzu. It has been said that the main difference between these three breeds was their coat, rather than their construction.

Unfortunately, the eunuchs kept their breeding records a close secret; no records or pedigrees appear to have been retained. All we have are visual images, for outstanding specimens were depicted on Imperial scrolls. Dogs considered less good specimens were smuggled out of the palace to be sold to Chinese noblemen or to foreigners, while others simply found their way into the marketplace. How sad the Empress would have been to know that after her death her precious 'Shih Tzu Kou' were dissipated.

THE EMPRESS'S FEEDING REGIME

The Empress laid down numerous rules for the palace dogs, one of which was that they had to be "dainty in their food", and it was by their fastidiousness that they could be recognised as Imperial dogs. Being fed the diet they were, no wonder they were fastidious!

"Sharks' fins and curlews' livers and breasts of quail, on these may it be fed, and for its drink give it the tea that is brewed from the spring buds of shrub that grow in the province of Hankow, or the milk of antelopes that pasture in the Imperial parks… Thus shall it preserve its integrity and self-respect, for the day of sickness let it be anointed with the clarified fat of a sacred leopard, and give it to drink a throstle's egg-shell full of the juice of the custard apple, in which has been dissolved three pinches of shredded rhinoceros horn, and apply to it piebald leeches."

There seems to be no record of how much the Empress's dogs enjoyed their food, but their diet was, thankfully, far removed from those of Chinese breeds in the West today.

OTHER OPINIONS AS TO THE ORIGIN

Author Brian Vesey Fitzgerald said he had always understood that in about 1650 three temple dogs were sent to China and that from these came the Shih Tzu. I do not know, though, how he obtained this information. He goes on to say that about 100 years later, the Dalai Lama gave some away to distinguished visitors who were Russians. He believes that until that time these dogs had always been His Holiness' special property.

However, these three dogs were stolen before they reached the border, and around the same time, during a civil upheaval, more disappeared from His Holiness' monastery, subsequently reappearing in various parts of the country. From then on, any long-coated dog bearing some resemblance to the original temple dog became an Apso. Vesey Fitzgerald says this was the end of the temple dog, but the start of the monastery dog and also of the caravan dog.

Another interesting viewpoint was put forward by L.A. Waddell in a record of the 1903-4 expedition to Lhasa: "They are fond of dogs, and especially favour the mongrel breed between the Lhassa Terrier and the Chinese Spaniel".

Dr Walter Young, in his monograph, *Some Canine Breeds of Asia*, believed there was evidence to support the claim that the "shock-headed variety of small dogs" so commonly seen in Peking, were in fact Tibetan in origin.

As in Britain, the Shih Tzu has had its fair share of confusion and controversy in China, too.

Chinese dog breeder in Lung Fussu market, Peking, early 20th century.

When the China Kennel Club was formed in Shanghai in 1923, all similar, small dogs of this general type were classified as Tibetan Poodles or Lhassa Terriers. Mr A. de C. Sowerby, a dog judge and also editor of the *Chinese Chronicle*, wrote in 1930, "It is our opinion that the Tibetan Lion Dog is the result of a cross between the Lhasa Terrier and Pekingese." He described how confusion had been caused in separating the breeds by the fact that all Tibetan breeds were grouped together. No guidance was laid down concerning the breeds and when he judged Lhassa Terriers (or Tibetan Poodles) in Shanghai, he had difficulty in deciding which dog

to put over another for this very reason. He also mentioned that the matter was exacerbated by the fact that the Tibetan dogs were called by so many different names.

Three years later he made a similar comment in the *China Journal of Shanghai*, saying he felt the Tibetan Lion Dog was the result of a cross between the Lhasa Terrier and Pekingese. The two breeds had been mixed, both in Tibet and in China, after being taken to and fro by envoys and officials. He understood the cross in Tibet that had been taken out of the country by way of India was called the Apso, while the cross in Peking was called the Tibetan Poodle or Lion Dog. He believed there was no doubt that the Tibetan dog had more of the Lhasa Terrier in it, while the Chinese cross had more of the Pekingese.

Certainly it is clear that the passage of dogs went both ways around, as is borne out in Suydam Cuttings' book, *The Fire Ox and Other Years*. In writing of his visit to Tibet in 1937, he mentions that dogs were occasionally taken into Tibet where they were highly appreciated. He says there was a pair of "beautiful Chinese dogs" in the "menagerie" of His Holiness the Dalai Lama. I do wonder, though, whether these may have been Pekingese, as I have come across several Pekingese dogs in Lhasa and in

Chinese Lion Dog, Peking, 1930s.

some of the Tibetan Buddhist monasteries in Nepal where they have, indeed, been highly prized.

As you can see, there have been various theories on how and when the Shih Tzu came about. I have travelled regularly to the Himalaya for 20 years, and now live here, but I have never yet found any actual proof that pure-bred Shih Tzu were presented to Chinese emperors over 300 years ago. If ever I do change my mind, I shall be the first to let you know…

THE HON MRS MCLAREN MORRISON

The Hon Mrs McLaren Morrison was a great exponent of Asian breeds, and in 1895 she wrote of the Japanese Spaniel and what she called the 'Nepalese Spaniel', saying the two closely resembled

each other in colouring, both generally black and white. The Nepalese dog was larger, though, but never bigger than the King Charles. She also mentioned that the Chinese Spaniel resembled them, except in colour, as they were of a deep orange or brindle. She said that although some were small enough to be put in the pocket, they were never so small as the Japanese Spaniels. Their coats, she said, were thick and flowing, and their faces rather short. She thought they were also called 'lion dogs'. They could, of course, have been Pekingese, but the fact that she describes the face as "rather short" might just indicate that they were actually Shih Tzu.

THE 1930s IN PEKING

In 1935 the Peking Kennel Club

published a thoroughly informative and charming booklet called the Lhassa Lion Dog. The name was established by the Peking KC to avoid the inevitable confusion that had arisen of the breed's various names for Tibetan Poodle, Poodle Terrier and Lhassa Terrier, which all seemed to refer to the same breed. The booklet was written by Madam Lu Zee Yuen Nee, a breeder with many years' experience and who had drawn her knowledge from various sources, including old paintings.

She writes of the Lhassa Lion Dog's courage and independence, not combative, but ever watchful, "and woe befall any daring to trespass"! She felt the independence of spirit was coupled with a quality of affection that was seldom equalled in any other breed.

She considered it was not a dog that liked to be pampered, for it preferred the home it made for itself over one that was made for it, but it did suffer illnesses if not protected from conditions that it was unable to naturally withstand. Madam Lu thought the breed slow in sight and in smell, but quick in hearing. She thought it not to be intolerant of caresses, but rather indifferent to them, for this was an aristocratic breed. However, she also said that the Lhassa Lion Dog was, in her opinion, timid but with an affectionate and gentle nature, liking to be with people and to be petted and cuddled. Perhaps different personalities emerged?

Even in the poorest quarters, the Lhassa Lion Dog was well cared for, indicative of the fine strain from which the breed had developed. They imposed their qualities on their surroundings. The breed rarely barked at strangers, and, when it moved, did so like a goldfish swimming in water.

Because yellow was China's Imperial colour, Madam Lu thought this the proper colour of the Lhassa Lion Dog. Dogs of a uniform colour were called 'Chin Chia Huang Pao', meaning 'golden armour, yellow gown'. But the yellow was more like the colour of a camel; if it were bright and glossy yellow, with stiff strands of hair, then it was not of pure breed type. Could this have indicated that the Pekingese was still showing through too strongly in some strains?

NAMING THE COLOURS

To mention all the Chinese names for colours could be confusing, but the English translations are simply enchanting, so I have to share them with you:

- A yellow coat and white neck were described as "golden cape with a white jade collar".
- A yellow coat with a white dome on the head was "golden basin upholding the moon".
- A dog with round, yellow patches was described as "whipping the embroidered balls".
- A yellow coat with a white tail was "white jade golden vase".
- A Lhassa Lion Dog with a yellow coat and white paws was "snowy mountain golden camel".
- Very pale dogs, cream or ivory white, were rare.
- A solid white dog was "one piece jade", but if it had blue eyes, it was "glass jade". Usually a cream coloured dog had pink eyes and nose.
- A solid black dog was "lump of ink".
- A black coat with a white dome was "jade tip".
- My favourite description is that of a black dog with white feet, "standing in snow".
- A black dog with a white tummy as well as white feet was "black clouds over snow".
- A dog with black back and white legs was "jade davenport".

Madame Lu Zee Yuen Lee's descriptions of the Lhassa Lion Dog, 1935.

LHASA APSO TRICKS

Tricks a Lhassa lion dog could do according to Madame Lu Zee Yuen Nee

- Sit up
- Pray
- Catch a ball
- Shake hands
- Hold a basket in the mouth
- Roll on the floor
- Sneeze
- Slide down a slope
- Bury an object
- Paw at a wash basin.

Madam Lu said the hair on black Lhassa Lion Dogs tended to be rather curly and stiff, sometimes with grey tips, but some dogs were grey with long, thick curly hair, and some black and white hair mixed in the coat. Dogs of this colour were called "old man in the grass raincoat".

Yellow or black dogs often had some white on their head or body, but never on the ears. A white dog often had black ears, and a black dog with "four eyes" (a Tibetan expression indicating tan points above the eyes, as found in many Tibetan Mastiffs) had yellow ears.

In dogs with mixed colours, the colours were to be evenly distributed, for if they were even on one side only this would be considered "one sided beauty".

Around the nose the hair was curled, and long hair covered the corners of the mouth; under the chin the hair was also long, covering the "apron". In general, the coat was "like a skein of yarn", on the legs it was meant to be a "like a waterfall", not like "petals of garlic". The leg hair came down to the toes and covered them, giving rise to the saying "seeing the legs but not the feet". There were five toes on each foot, in "the shape of mountain ranges".

Many of the other descriptions given tie in closely with the Shih Tzu we know so well today: the mouth "flat and short", the nose "flat" with a stop at the bridge of the nose. There were to be bunches of hair growing around the nose, if it were lacking, this was a fault. Small eyes were also a fault – "they were to be 'big, protruding, and brilliant". One can only presume that there was then in Peking a problem with broken pigment, as the eyelids were to be smooth and of one colour. Teeth were to be "all inside the lips and not protruding, except when a dog expresses joy". Protruding teeth were a fault.

As the booklet continues, there was evidence of different 'types', some of which had been bred in Tibet and some in Peking, for we read: "Lhassa Lion Dogs should be bred in Peiping. (Tibetan bred dogs are heavy and more ferocious, while Peiping bred ones are light and more gentle.)"

CUSTOMARY NAMES FOR LION DOGS IN PEKING IN THE 1930s

- Ting Erh – top child (because it has a white dome)
- Chueh Tse – tangerine (a dog of yellow colour)
- Hsing Erh – apricot colour
- Li Tse – brown colour
- Hsiao Hei – small black
- Yu Tse – jade child

- Mien Hua – cotton
- Hsiao Hsueh Pai Tse – small snow white child
- Yang Tse – lamb child (for a white dog)
- Lai Tse – come child (used for a dog taken home from elsewhere)

- Hsiao Tse – a boy (a favourite name for a male)
- Niu Tse – a girl (a favourite name for a bitch)
- Hsiao Ping – peace (usually used for dogs of mixed colours)
- Hsi Tzi – happiness

CHINESE VIEWS ON DOGS

China has changed in recent decades, and so has the attitude of many Chinese people, but in earlier years the Chinese thought of dogs as having the same passions and feelings as men. This made it easy for them to believe that dogs could change into men, and men into dogs. A fascinating practice was carried out in 701 when the Imperial Guards had a duty to bark like dogs on special occasions. This was done to drive away evil spirits or ghosts. When a foreigner arrived at court, there was no special number of barks they had to give, but when the Chinese Emperor drove up, it had to be two.

Traditionally, the Chinese have always considered that a stray dog coming into the home is a sign of good luck for the family, and future prosperity. A dog is also believed to have magical healing powers. It was possible to buy pieces of paper stamped with the head of a dog from the temple keeper, and these cost no mean sum. The charmed paper was taken home and burned and could cause someone to be obedient to the will of another. In more extreme cases, it was believed it could cause someone to become stupid, or even to die. This came about by the ashes of the burned charm being placed in the unwitting recipient's food, in his tea, or else they were smeared on his clothing.

But it was not all plain sailing for the person who had purchased the charm, for sometimes it could recoil on the person himself, or indeed on some poor individual who just happened to be near at the time!

A similar charm was used by ladies of easy virtue if they wanted a rich guest to return to them. The lady would mix the ashes in the gentleman's drink, or alternatively, she could burn it after he had gone, uttering words indicating that, like a dog, he would return.

Lastly it is worth mentioning that a dog born with five toes on all four feet was believed to have been lucky, and a good specimen. This bodes well for Shih Tzu, for several have dewclaws on all four feet!

A BUDDHIST VIEWPOINT

Those who follow Buddhism believe in reincarnation, so tend to treat their dogs with greater kindness than do other Asian cultures. Buddhists believe that they may well have been a dog in a previous life, or that they may return as a dog in a future life. Re-birth on the human plane is not a frequent occurrence. Every living being is treated with respect and Buddhists do not take life; even a flea is carefully removed and placed elsewhere, rather than killed.

But a Buddhist viewpoint that is less easy for us modern-day dog owners to accept is that because they do not kill, neither do they put kindly to sleep a dog who is suffering or in pain. This is something with which I, personally, have found difficult, but have been told that His Holiness the Dalai Lama has now said that putting a dog kindly to

Buddhist Lion Masque, Peking 1914.

Tang and Lung-Fu-Ssu, owned by Miss Hutchins.

sleep for a good reason is "a black deed with a white motive". I do so hate having a dog put to sleep and always leave it until the very last moment, but this has served to clear my conscience a little.

Dogs that are taken on sacred pilgrimages and circumambulations of holy places are believed to be a receptacle for those evil spirits that might have displeased the dog's master. It has been said that when a dog's master died en route, as sometimes happened, the dog would continue the circumambulation until he, too, died. In Tibetan Buddhist culture, the life of the dog is closely interwoven with that of man for his body is used to give warmth, his coat spun to make clothing, while his bark serves to warn his master of intruders. It is

considered ill-mannered to suggest that a nomad should sell a dog, for even if he may make a present of a puppy to friends, he will never part with an adult dog.

THE SHIH TZU LEAVES CHINA

In 1919 Lady Brownrigg married her husband, who was later to become General Sir Douglas Brownrigg. While he was posted to the North China Command, the couple managed to acquire their first Shih Tzu. They had heard of 'Tibetan Lion Dogs' or 'Shock-dogs' owned by the Emperors, and that they had been given to them as tribute gifts by Tibet's Dalai Lama. The Brownriggs lived in Peking and believed the best ones could be found there. They had seen a small black-and-white dog that took their fancy and determined

to obtain one that was similar.

The first bitch they acquired sadly died in whelp, but in 1927 they found another black-and-white bitch, with the help of Madam Wellington Koo. Named Shu-ssa, she was small, with a white 'apple mark' on her head and a black patch on the root of her tail and on her side. Her large, expressive eyes and her hair sticking out around her face made her look like a fluffy baby owl, or a chrysanthemum. Shu-ssa had a thick coat and her tail was curled quite tightly over her back.

Tibetan Lion Dogs, though, were not generally seen in public places for they were primarily kept inside the homes of the Chinese, and in their courtyards. The Palace eunuchs, she knew, had some, and a few had been bred by French and Russian people living in China. The Brownriggs wanted to find another parti-coloured dog as a mate for Shu-ssa, and, during their search, they came across some large, coarse dogs with black or dark grey coats, while a few others were gold.

A Dr Cernier had a small, rather lightly built black-and-white male, with a good tail carriage and a straight, soft coat. He was considered very active, a great character and a sportsman, added to which he was a proven sire. When Dr Cernier returned home to France, the dog, named Hibou, came into the possession of the Brownriggs.

Another dog that appeared on the scene around the same time

Hibou and Yangtze, owned by Mrs Brownrigg.

was Miss Hutchings' Lung-Fu-ssu, who was whelped in 1926. This was a heavier dog, white-and-black, with a coarser, rather wavy coat and a rather loose tail. When Miss Hutchins returned to England in 1930, she brought with her Lung-fu-ssu, a bitch called Mei Mei and also the Brownriggs' two dogs. Sadly, Mei Mei was killed by a Sealyham Terrier after she came out of quarantine. These dogs were still known as Tibetan Lion Dogs and their weights ranged from just over 12 lbs (5.5 kgs) to 14 lbs 9 oz (6.65 kgs). Lady Brownrigg knew there were other, smaller dogs in China, but these were not used for breeding.

Shu-ssa, mated to Hibou, produced her first litter in quarantine in April of 1930. When puppies could be released from quarantine at the age of

eight weeks, Miss Hutchins had one of the puppies, Tai-tai, who went on to produce several Shih Tzu litters. From that first litter, two puppies, Ting and Popen, went to Lady Brownrigg's parents, General and Mrs Jefferies, and a bitch went to a childhood friend, Mrs Robert Bruce, who lived in Scotland.

The following year, in 1931, Lady Brownrigg returned to England and also that year Shu-ssa produced her second litter, this time mated to Lung-fu-ssu. In 1932 she had her third and last litter, which was a repeat mating to Hibou.

THE LHASA APSO CONNECTION
Around the same time as the Brownriggs were involved with the Lhasa Lion Dogs in China, Colonel and Mrs Irma Bailey were

involved in acquiring Lhasa Apsos in Tibet. Colonel Bailey had taken over from Sir Charles Bell as political officer for Tibet in 1921. By 1928 the Baileys had brought back six Apsos to England; five of these were descendents of their original pair, which had been presented to Mrs Bailey in 1922, when she was living in Sikkim, on the Tibetan border.

Mrs Bailey had already observed that the 'Lhasa Terriers' in the interior of Tibet and near the Indian border were generally more terrier-like than those found near the Chinese border, where they tended to have shorter legs, shorter muzzles and were rounder in eye. One cannot help but think that the latter may well have been Shih Tzu.

Several small long-coated dogs had now arrived in Britain, so the

Cheltenham Show, 1933. Before the breeds were sorted out, Lhasa Apso and Shih Tzu competed together. L-R: Lady Brownrigg with Hibou, Yangtse and Shu-Ssa, Miss Hutchins with Lung-Fu-Ssu and Tang, General Sir Douglas Brownrigg with Hzu-Hsi, and Miss Marjorie Wild with one of her Lhasa Apsos.

'Apso and Lion Dog Club' was formed. This club was recognised by the Kennel Club and held its first show at the West of England Ladies Kennel Club Show in 1933. Although all dogs were exhibited together, it was immediately apparent that the dogs varied tremendously, especially in length of foreface. Colonel Bailey was the judge and he made no secret of the fact that he thought the dogs from China were of a different breed, saying he thought they had been crossed with the Pekingese.

THE 'BATTLE OF THE NOSES' BEGAN

Correspondence flew hither and thither across Britain. In 1934 General Brownrigg wrote to Lieut. Colonel Bailey explaining how he had come across his dogs and how, in 1929, he had heard Mrs Bailey's name mentioned for the first time as both the Brownriggs and Mrs Bailey had admired the very same dog, Brownie, in Peking. They later learned that Mrs Bailey had imported dogs to Britain and had assumed they were similar to their own, this supposition having been based on their mutual admiration of Brownie, who was not for sale.

Twice the Brownriggs went to visit Mrs Bailey, who had already registered her dogs as Lhasa Apsos, but among her dogs they found only two puppies with short noses similar to those of their own dogs. On the second visit they took along photographs of their own dogs, and Mrs Bailey wrote across the back of one of

the photos that she considered them to be Apsos. Armed with this photograph, the Brownriggs went to the Kennel Club and got their dogs registered as Apsos.

Colonel Brownrigg said that all that was now in the past and there was no turning back, so suggested that they tried to get the Kennel Club to register both types under the name of Apso, but differentiate them by the names 'Apsos, Chinese Type' and 'Apsos, Tibetan Type'. The KC, however, advised them to separate their dogs entirely from the Lhasa Apso and to register them as Shih Tzu, to which the Brownriggs agreed.

Then arose some contention as to whether the Shih Tzu, when registered as such, would still be considered a Tibetan breed. There was once again heated debate as many owners of Shih Tzu refused to drop the word 'Tibetan' and continued to refer to their breed as 'Tibetan Lion Dog'. By now the Tibetan Breeds Association had been formed and wrote to the Kennel Club protesting that the word 'Tibetan' should not be used for a type of dog that may originally have been Tibetan but which had so long been bred in China that it had lost its original true Tibetan character.

In September of 1934 the *Kennel Gazette* carried the announcement: "The application to change the title of the Apso and Lion Dog Club to Shih Tzu (Tibetan Lion Dog) Club, was granted".

But the problems did not stop

Controversy surrounded formal recognition of the Shih Tzu.

Ch. Ta Chi of Taishan: The breed's first Champion.

there. The Tibetan Breeds Association had always maintained that the Lhasa Apso was the true Tibetan Lion Dog, and as the name was such an attractive one it was felt that in the interests of harmony it should be discarded by all parties. There are pages and pages of correspondence, which I shall refrain from detailing here, suffice it to say that in February 1935 the club became known simply as the Shih Tzu Club.

EARLY DAYS OF THE SHIH TZU IN BRITAIN

Miss Hutchins and the Brownriggs co-operated closely regarding the breeding of Shih Tzu in the UK; they detailed all important facts about every puppy born and inspected litters whenever possible. With General Brownrigg as Treasurer and Lady Brownrigg as Secretary, the Shih Tzu Club grew in strength.

By 1939 a total of 183 Shih Tzu had been registered with the Kennel Club and 1940 was a very important year for the breed, as it was granted a separate register, instead of being registered under 'Any Other Variety'. Nonetheless, the Shih Tzu did not become eligible for Challenge Certificates until after the war.

During the war years Lady Brownrigg was much involved with Red Cross work; wool from Shih Tzu coat groomings was made into yarn and used to knit articles that were sold in aid of the Red Cross. It was a struggle to preserve the breed, as breeding practically ceased; like other breeds, the Shih Tzu was at risk of dying out. At the end of the war, a few of the original breeders bred from their remaining stock and new imports, and they resumed their showing activities.

But numbers were low, so, to preserve the breed, all available stock had to be used for breeding, regardless of its quality. This is why some of the dogs of the post-war era are very varied in quality; there was an increase in size and many Shih Tzu produced were too large. In 1945 only two Shih Tzu were registered with the Kennel Club, one of which was Ta Chi of Taisha (Sui-Yan x Madam Ko of Taishan) who in 1949 was to become the breed's first Champion. Owned and bred by Lady Brownrigg, she was descended from the Norwegian import, Choo-Choo, from Tashi of Chouette and from the first British imports. Even today she is held in high regard and many feel she has been one of the most typical specimens of the breed.

Mr and Mrs Bode had first come into contact with the breed

when living in Persia, but when they returned to the UK in 1945, none of their dogs came back with them. In 1948 Mrs Bode managed to acquire a dog and a bitch, Sing Tzu of Shebo and Shebo Tsemo of Lhakang; later they were joined by Schunde, a black son of Ishuh Tzu who had been imported from China.

Indeed several Shih Tzu had been imported prior to the war years, but many were not bred from. Choo Choo came to Her Majesty The Queen from Norway in 1933, Fu Tzu and Nui San, bred by the Countess d'Anjou in 1937 were brought from China by Mrs Audrey Fowler in 1937, but they left no progeny. Ming, a black-and-white dog, came in from China in 1939. Three others came in from Canada, two died, but Tashi of Chouette appears to have introduced liver pigmentation.

Following the war, in 1948, the gold-brindle and white Ishuh Tzu was imported from China and this line appears to have been the first to introduce solid colours. A dog, Wuffles, and a bitch, Mai-Ting, were also imported from

Princess Margaret Rose holding Choo Choo.
Photo courtesy: Studio Lisa.

China, although their ancestry was unknown. When back in England the two were mated together and produced a black-and-white bitch.

THE POST-WAR SHIH TZU
The Shih Tzu Club once more became active when the war years were over. Few puppies had been

produced, but already the breed had produced its first Champion and during the 1950s several new breeders became involved. In 1950 Mr and Mrs Kenneth Rawlings appeared in the Shih Tzu show rings with Perky Ching of the Mynd and their Antarctica kennel influenced the breed both in coat quality and in presentation. The next year, Mrs Widdrington's Lhakang kennel produced its first Champion in Sheba Tsemo of Lhakang. Along with Lady Brownrigg's Taishans, the Lhakang and Antarctica dogs were highly successful in the breed over the coming decade.

THE SHIH TZU IN AMERICA
As in Britain, the Shih Tzu and Lhasa Apso were confused in the USA during the early years. In the mid-1930s the American Kennel Club (AKC) had received an application to register a Shih Tzu, but made the statement "the Lhassa Terrier and Shih Tzu are one and the same breed".

Correspondence went back and forth across the Atlantic, the differences between the two breeds being very clearly pointed out by the Secretary of the Tibetan Breeds Association in Britain.

Mr and Mrs Patrick Morgan, who had obtained their Shih Tzu in Peking and lived in Canada, wrote several articles about Shih Tzu and Lhasa Apsos for the American press in the 1930s, helping to make the breeds better understood in the US. They pointed out that the separation between the two breeds had slowed up recognition in other countries and that England should clearly state what it had done so that others might know.

Dogs that had been registered correctly in Britain as Shih Tzu were exported to the USA where they were registered incorrectly as Lhasa Apsos. This has indeed had a long-term detrimental effect on the latter for the confusion continued until the 1950s, resulting in many Lhasa Apsos that were bred in the USA in those relatively early years carrying a high proportion of Shih Tzu blood.

PEKINGESE CROSS IN THE UK

Within the Pekingese world, Miss Freda Evans was a breeder of high repute. She later became involved in Shih Tzu, and, although a newcomer to the breed, she believed she could improve on certain faults that she felt were creeping in. She considered the breed too closely

Am. Ch. Jungfaltets Jung-Wu, descends from three Chinese imports, and helped to establish the breed in the USA.

in-bred and recognised problems of over-size, narrow heads, snipey muzzles and long noses, along with evidence of terrier legs, narrow fronts, loose-jointedness, poor coats, near-set eyes and 'bad carriage'. These, though, were Miss Evans' opinions and were not necessarily held by other breeders of the time, who were much more experienced in their breed than Miss Evans.

Miss Evans' plan was to introduce a Pekingese cross to the Shih Tzu breed, which understandably did not go down well with some, though others looked at it in a more favourable light, thinking that a Pekingese cross would bring in fewer faults than using an imported Shih Tzu

of unknown pedigree. However, the crossing took place without consultation with the Shih Tzu Club, indeed Miss Evans did not write to the club explaining her motives until after the birth of the puppies, so this was a highly controversial move, to say the very least!

The dogs used for the cross mating were a black Shih Tzu, Elfann Fenling of Yram, and a black-and-white Pekingese, Philadelphia Suti T'Sun of Elfann, described as "a good little dog with a perfect mouth". But he also had rather straight legs, which was one of the reasons why he was chosen as the stud. The cross was correctly registered with the KC and extreme care

Introducing Pekingese bloodlines to the Shih Tzu was the subject of debate for many years.

was taken in the integration of the offspring into Shih Tzu breeding programmes. However, this controversial mating was a subject of much debate for many a long year. Only one bitch puppy of each succeeding generation was mated back to a Shih Tzu until the third generation, when six puppies were registered, four of which were bred from. Still they were technically crossbreeds, but their progeny would be eligible for first-class registration as pure Shih Tzu. Using this stock, extensive breeding was then carried out up and down Britain and, in due course, the majority of kennels in the UK had some of this blood somewhere in their pedigrees, for it was difficult to avoid in-breeding without actually incorporating it.

Exports from the UK also carried this line, especially to Sweden where Fu-Ling of Clytsvale, exported in 1958, became a strong stud influence. The dog that went on to become one of the most successful English-bred dogs on the continent at that time was Ch. Golden Peregrine of Elfann, who was exported to Italy where he gained his international title.

In time, the breed did become more uniform in size; the really large specimens were rarely found and the small ones were usually not below 12 lbs (5.5 kgs). Nonetheless, there is still a very wide weight range for Shih Tzu. Chinese visitors to England, knowing that large specimens had not been kept in the Imperial Palace, have criticised the size of British dogs. It appears that both the Pekingese influence and Swedish lines were largely responsible for reducing size, and the smaller dogs were generally of sounder construction than they had previously been.

Not only did the Pekingese cross cause controversy, so did the fact that the Lhakang kennel began to specialise in breeding 'tinies'. These two matters combined were sufficient to split both the breed and the club in two. This was a breed that had been noted for its ease of whelping, and some thought that the breeding of very small Shih Tzu would bring with it whelping problems. Lady Brownrigg wrote to the KC imploring them not to allow such a small size, but her request fell on deaf ears for they accepted a revised Breed Standard allowing 'tinies' but not miniatures. Lady Brownrigg then asked if there could be a division into two size ranges, but this was not allowed. However, weight classes were put on at shows so that the smaller specimens might be accommodated.

A private club was set up in 1956 with the aim of promoting the smaller size. At first the KC did not allow it to have its own title, but, after modifying its aims, the KC eventually agreed and the Manchu Shih Tzu Club came into being. During the 1960s registrations rose steadily, as did exports abroad, most of which went to the USA, but in the space of 10 years over a 100 went to Japan, where the Shih Tzu became one of the numerically strongest breeds.

A significant moment came in British Shih Tzu history when Ken and Betty Rawlings took the accolade of Best in Show at the

Ch. Easy Rider at Huxlor: Making his mark in the show ring today.

Ch. Huxlor Trigger Happy: This dog, who has American bloodlines, has been a hugely successful sire in the UK.

West of England Ladies' Kennel Association's Championship Show with Ch. Pan-Mao Chen of Antarctica, in 1963. In this same eventful decade, a Championship title was awarded to one of the smaller Shih Tzu for the first time. This was Ch. Tien Memsahib, who weighed just 10 lbs (4.5 kgs).

So from its early beginnings in China, the breed worked its way around the world, and even back to Asia again. Despite turbulent times, the Shih Tzu has taken its place in the history books – even the 'tinies' – and has become a much-admired breed that could hold its own amongst the very strongest competition. Still the Shih Tzu graces show rings all over the world, and has won many a high accolade across the globe.

A SHIH TZU FOR YOUR LIFESTYLE

Chapter 3

Whatever kind of pet you have decided should join your household, it entails enormous responsibility. Even a goldfish needs feeding, its water changing and keeping clean, while a rabbit is even more time-consuming, especially if it is a breed like an Angora. Cats need a lot of care, too, but they are much more independent than dogs, who, in the main, are totally dependent upon their owner. And a Shih Tzu… well, with that coat it's a dog and half to look after!

A Shih Tzu may be small, but his coat is very demanding, whether it is kept long or short. This breed has a big personality but is very easy to get along with, so if this is the breed you have selected, you have chosen well, provided you are prepared to put in the time and effort to keep your Shih Tzu happy and healthy, both mentally and physically.

MAKING THE COMMITMENT
By the time you are ready to make the commitment to own a Shih Tzu, you should already have done an enormous amount of homework. From the very outset you must be certain that this is really the right breed for you and your family. There is no turning back later, so there are numerous questions you will need to have asked yourself.

Can you devote sufficient time to a Shih Tzu's coat care? The coat will take a lot of time and care if you are to maintain it in good condition, even if you have decided to keep him as a family pet in 'puppy trim' rather than as a show dog. Ideally, trimming should be done professionally, so unless you are already a skilled groomer, grooming costs must be taken into consideration in either situation.

The length and density of coat, and the fact that it does not shed, means regular grooming is an absolute must, especially if the coat is kept long. Although the Shih Tzu does not shed his coat, the long coat and wet feet can cause a lot of extra housework after your dog has come running in from the garden on a winter's day.

There are, of course, other costs associated with dogs, but we shall look at these more specifically as we progress through this chapter.

WHO WILL LOOK AFTER YOUR DOG?
If you go out to work, even only for a few hours a day, you must consider who will look after your Shih Tzu while you are not at home. In this day and age, more and more people work from

home – a situation that is ideal for Shih Tzu ownership. You can be assured that your canine friend will keep you good company throughout the day; the only problem being that if you sit at a computer all day, as I do, there will almost always be a Shih Tzu reclining under your seat, running into the danger of your chair wheels rolling over the coat, removing clumps of hair!

If you work away from home on a full-time basis, you must be realistic and not take on the ownership of a dog unless you have someone responsible to look after him for at least a few hours each day. A dog may be left for two or three hours each day, but not any longer. It could be that a member of your household will be at home while you are out at work, or a professional dog sitter or walker could be employed. But this, of course, will involve additional expense, and the cost may be prohibitive if it is something that is needed on a regular basis.

Some people are able to take their dogs to work with them and this, too, could be a very good arrangement, particularly as the Shih Tzu has a personality conducive to meeting people. If you do find yourself in this fortunate situation, it is best to

Taking on a dog of any breed is a big commitment, but a high maintenance breed, such as the Shih Tzu, requires dedication.

introduce your Shih Tzu to the routine while he still young so that he will adapt easily to his 'work schedule'. But remember that all dogs, although they may enjoy the routine, must have frequent opportunities to go for short walks and to relieve themselves. Puppies, of course, need toilet breaks more often than adults. The last thing you want is for your dog to disgrace himself in the office – he may never be invited again!

HOW MUCH DOES IT COST?

If you wish to buy a Shih Tzu puppy with a good pedigree, the cost will be fairly substantial. It may be slightly more if you aim to have a show dog rather than a pet, but both should have been

raised to the same high standards, so there may not be a very great difference. It is probably best to ring a breed club secretary to get some advice on price before you start to make your enquiries. The secretary may also know who has puppies available at the time of your enquiry, so will be able to point you in the right direction.

It is imperative that you purchase from a reputable breeder. The Kennel Club now offers an Accredited Breeder Scheme, but there are many good and experienced breeders who choose not to take part in this for very valid reasons. On the other hand, there are several not-so-good breeders who, although 'Accredited', manage to slip through the net. You will really need to use your own intuitive powers when choosing a breeder. Make sure you ask the right questions, and expect to be asked many questions in return.

Remember that, inevitably, there are some bad breeders out there, who are 'in it for the money'. So you may well find a breeder asking a high price for their stock, even though little or no thought has gone into the breeding, and probably little into the care of the puppies. If, for any reason, you are unsure about whether the breeder you are considering is reputable, do not let your heart rule your head. Simply walk away, which will hopefully discourage the breeder from trying to earn money from producing future litters.

When good breeders are setting a price for their puppies, they will have taken into consideration the many expenses they have incurred. These will include health checks on the dam prior to mating, a stud fee, which can be considerable when using a health-checked dog of high quality, veterinary costs that may have been involved prior to and post whelping, and possibly vaccination fees, at least for the first vaccine, this depending upon the age at which the puppies leave home. Added to this there will be Kennel Club registration fees, and it is certainly to be hoped that the puppy you buy will be KC registered. Puppies that are not KC registered will cost considerably less, but there will be a reason why this is the case – usually a negative one – so, as a purchaser, you will need an honest explanation.

You will also have to bear in mind the upkeep cost of your Shih Tzu. Apart from the grooming costs involved, there will also be the cost of food, veterinary bills and other incidentals, such as bedding, collars and leads, and maybe even a little coat to wear when out walking in inclement weather. Even the special elastic bands you use to tie up your Shih Tzu's head hair will add to the bill. You may decide to take out veterinary insurance, but this will not cover the cost of routine vaccinations.

FOOD

There are so very many different ways of feeding a dog, and the cost will depend to a large extent on the type of diet you choose. The Shih Tzu is only a small

Breeding a Shih Tzu litter is an expensive business, and this will be reflected in the purchase price of puppies.

breed, so costs are not so much as feeding one of the giant breeds, such as a Mastiff. Nonetheless, food costs do mount up over a year, and this should never be overlooked when calculating how much it will cost you to keep your dog. *For information on feeding a Shih Tzu, see Chapter Five: The Best of Care.*

EQUIPMENT

Food bowls, grooming equipment, collars, leads, bedding and even 'poo bags' all cost money. My advice is that any items that can be used long term should be of the highest quality so that you get as much life out of them as possible. The initial outlay will be a little higher but, over time, these will most probably turn out to be cost-saving. Stainless-steel feeding and water bowls, for example, do not cost much more than ceramic bowls, but apart from being much more hygienic, they will last almost forever.

TRAINING

Training need not cost money if you are able to train a dog yourself, but you may want to take your Shih Tzu along to training classes – ringcraft for a show dog and obedience for a pet. Most of these classes are very inexpensive, but there are also some private training establishments, which cost more. Most of these run six-, eight- or 10-week courses, for which you have to pay a course fee.

Some training classes help dogs to work toward the Kennel Club Good Citizen scheme, in which there are Bronze, Silver and Gold awards, for which you and your dog can aim. These make very good sense and provide evidence that your Shih Tzu is indeed a 'Good Citizen'.

Because of the Shih Tzu's good nature, you are unlikely to have difficulty with temperament or behavioural problems, but if you do, you may decide on one-to-one training, which will be much more costly. But remember, you must be trained as well as your dog, so there is no point in sending your dog away for training. This simply won't work long-term, and when your dog returns home you will almost certainly be back at square one again.

Other forms of training include agility, obedience and heelwork to music.

For more information, see Chapter Six: Training and Behaviour.

VETERINARY BILLS

The Shih Tzu is a long-lived breed, which means you and your friend will spend more happy years together than is the case with many other breeds. However, veterinary costs are likely to rise during the closing years of your dog's life.

Occasionally, Shih Tzu get 'dry eye' when they get into their teens, so the eye needs to be kept artificially moist. In mild cases, artificial 'tear drops' may be sufficient to keep the problem at bay, but in more severe cases a special tube of ointment is needed from your vet. Keeping the Shih Tzu's hair carefully tied up on top of the head will help to alleviate the situation, should it arise, and may also help to allay

Fortunately, the Shih Tzu is a healthy, long-lived breed, but you need to be able to cope with veterinary bills if the need arises.

Keeping a Shih Tzu in full coat demands time, money and patience.

the onset, as this prevents irritation to the eye.

For more information on health care, see Chapter Eight: Happy and Healthy.

INSURANCE

Insurance is not an inexpensive item by any means and will run well into three figures each year. Price usually depends on the size of the dog, so a Shih Tzu tends to be at the lower end of the scale. If you have only one dog, or perhaps a couple, insurance is an extremely good idea, but do shop around to see which companies offer the best deals.

Remember, too, that the cheapest is not always the best.

Usually you will still have to pay for minor treatment and generally an excess of the first £30 ($45) or so for more costly work by your vet. You are asked to put in a claim for treatment and you will be reimbursed at a later date. Some insurance policies also cover third-party injury, or damage to someone else's property. As Shih Tzu are not hunting dogs and not large enough to cause too much damage, you will never have to claim for these, with luck, but it's always reassuring to keep in the

back of your mind should the unforeseen happen.

GROOMING

Grooming is a highly important aspect of canine maintenance for the Shih Tzu and will involve cost in terms of both money and time, especially the latter.

You will definitely need to set aside a place in the home for grooming. If you have a utility room off your kitchen, this is probably ideal. Obviously there will be a considerable outlay in terms of equipment, but if you keep your Shih Tzu in short coat, usually known as 'pet trim', you

The male Shih Tzu is quick to mature and may show interest in bitches from as early as seven months.

We have already discussed some of differences between dogs and bitches, but which you choose is really a matter of personal preference. Within each litter, dogs tend to be a little larger than bitches. When they have reached maturity, dogs lift their legs, whilst bitches squat to do their toilet. From a practical point of view, the gardeners amongst you may favour your flowerbeds over a pristine lawn, or vice versa!

As any male dog reaches maturity, he is ready to pursue any bitch that happens to be in season. A Shih Tzu's interest in bitches can even commence from the age of seven months, so if you have a male, never underestimate his sexual desires and prowess! Bitches, on the other hand, are usually only receptive to males for roughly four days at the height of their season; the rest of the time they will make it clear they are not ready for his desires. Leading up to a season, and also afterwards, a bitch's hormones affect her mood, so your Shih Tzu bitch will appreciate 'kid glove' treatment around this time.

If you have both sexes in your canine family, there must be some sort of provision for the two to be kept apart when your bitch is in season. If you have more than one bitch, bear in mind that when one is in season, she will often 'bring the other/s in', so at least you will be able to get the difficult time over in a relatively short while. After this, household life can return to its usual blissful

will cut down on these costs a little, although you will most probably also have professional grooming bills, which will mount up.

When selecting a professional groomer, do make sure they understand the nature of the Shih Tzu's coat and have suitable experience. There may be a parlour to which you can take your pet, but some operate a mobile service, where they bath and groom your dog in your own home, which you and your dog may prefer.

THE RIGHT PUPPY

Hopefully the Shih Tzu who joins you will be Kennel Club registered, and his breeder will be a member of at least one of the breed clubs, indicating that he or she abides by the club's Code of Ethics. If you wish to show your Shih Tzu, it essential that the puppy is KC registered and the price will reflect this. As I have already said, many not-so-good breeders whose puppies are not registered still charge high prices, but an unregistered puppy should be considerably cheaper.

normality in your personal Shih Tzu world.

FINDING A BREEDER

Unless you know someone in the breed, the obvious first port of call when you begin to look for a Shih Tzu puppy is to contact the secretary of one of the specialist breed clubs, either the one that is most local to you, or one of the national clubs, such as the Shih Tzu Club or the Manchu Shih Tzu Society in the UK, and the American Shih Tzu Club in the US. Contact details change from time to time, so if you have difficulty knowing where to find details, I suggest you call the Kennel Club/AKC. If you have access to the internet, most clubs have their own websites, so if you just type in 'Shih Tzu' and scroll down, you will find the clubs listed.

The secretaries of clubs will generally be able to put you in touch with breeders who have litters, or who have bitches due to whelp very soon. The advantage of speaking to breed club secretaries is that they know and understand the breed, and have at least some knowledge of who the breeders are. Seeking advice through a less-specialised source does not have this advantage.

Be aware that breeders will not usually allow you to view the puppies at a very young age, probably not until they are four weeks or older, when their eyes are open and they are starting to walk around and play. However keen you may be to see your

If you opt for a bitch, you will have to cope with her seasonal cycle.

potential new puppy, do not be over-anxious, for unless you are an experienced breeder, you are unlikely to know what traits you should be looking for in a young whelp. Under no circumstances should you arrange to collect a puppy that is less than eight weeks old. Many good breeders do not allow their puppies to leave until they are about 10 weeks, but eight is the absolute minimum.

When visiting a litter, it is unlikely that the puppies' sire will be available for you to see, unless

he is owned by the breeder, which may be the case in one of the better-known kennels where a number of Shih Tzu are kept and where successful breeding lines have been established. In any event, you should be able to see a photograph of the stud dog and find out details of his show career. If the breeder has a website, you may also be able to view pictures of the puppies, their dam and possibly their sire on the internet, which will give you some idea of colouring at least.

You will usually have to wait until the litter is at least four weeks old before you can book a visit.

VIEWING THE LITTER

First of all, I would like to stress that you must be honest both with the breeder and yourself. If you try to cover up some important facts about your own home situation, you may end up with the wrong puppy out of the litter, or, indeed, a Shih Tzu may not be the breed for you at all. If, for example, you know you have a particularly unruly child, you really must say so. It may be difficult to admit to, but for the sake of the puppy and long-term harmony in the household, this must be discussed.

Having said that, when you go to visit a litter for the first time, on the assumption that there will also be a second visit, it is sensible to leave the children at home. If you have a partner, both of you should visit, as the puppy must be suitable for you both, and the breeder will certainly want to meet you. Children can be very persuasive, so without them you will probably be able to make a more considered decision as to whether this is the right litter from which to buy. On the second visit, the children should go along with you so that both you and the breeder can see how they interact.

Do try to be on time for your appointment, for unless you have had a litter, you will not know how important timing is. The breeder will be anxious that you see them clean and tidy, and puppies 'pee' and 'poo' a lot. The breeder may even have timed your visit to coincide with a mealtime, and puppies' routine cannot be thrown out of sync at this young age. If you are delayed en route for some unavoidable reason, please telephone the breeder to explain; I can assure you this will be much appreciated.

Keep in mind that the dam of the litter may be protective of her puppies, especially if they are still young, so only approach them if the breeder feels it is right for you to do so. She will not want their dam to be upset and, of course, there is always a risk of infection, so never visit a litter if you have been exposed to a possible

SHOW PROSPECT

If you are looking for a Shih Tzu as a show dog, you will probably need to be guided by the breeder as to which one has the most potential, but always remember that nothing can be certain. You can never buy 'a show puppy', but you can buy one 'with show potential'. Puppies can change as they grow up, and faults in construction may not show up until later.

Breeding lines develop differently, so the breeder will have the very best idea of what puppy may develop correctly or otherwise in maturity. Many a promising puppy has shattered his owner's dreams when something has gone dramatically wrong as the different parts of his anatomy have developed.

It takes an expert eye to assess show potential in a puppy.

infection, and make sure your hands and clothes are clean. You may be asked to take off your shoes before entering the home and to wash your hands again upon arrival; again, this is understandable with young pups around.

It goes without saying that all the puppies in the litter should look in the best of health, with no runny eyes or tacky bottoms. Their coats will still be quite short, but they should have an abundance of clean hair, and their tummies should be rounded though not too bulbous, as this may be an indication of worms. Their environment should be scrupulously clean. It may be interesting to note that a good growth of hair on the stomach is an indication that the puppy will become heavily coated in adulthood.

Regardless of whether you are aiming to take home a puppy as a pet or for the show ring, your intention must be that the puppy will remain with you for life. This means it is imperative that you completely fall in love with the puppy. If you have any reservations at all, then this may not be the Shih Tzu for you – or the Shih Tzu breed may not be the right one to tick all the boxes.

GETTING TO KNOW THE BREEDER

Before visiting the litter of puppies, you will probably have had a long chat with the breeder on the phone, during which time questions have been fired from both sides. Many good breeders turn away potential puppy buyers at this stage, so if you have been

The breeder will ask searching questions to make sure you can offer a suitable home to a Shih Tzu puppy.

invited to visit, there is an increased chance that the breeder may consider you a suitable owner.

It is important, too, that you feel confident with the breeder. He or she must be someone you can trust and to whom you can turn if you have any questions at all about the health and welfare of your Shih Tzu puppy throughout his life. As time progresses, you will get to understand your dog's habits and ways, and you will learn to understand if he is perhaps feeling 'off colour'. But the first few days and weeks can be difficult, and you do not want to feel that you have no one to turn to. It is important that you have

someone only a telephone call away if you feel you need to ascertain that what your puppy is doing is normal for the breed. You may be having problems with the feeding routine, which is again something you should be able to discuss freely with the breeder.

Although you will plan to keep the puppy for the duration of its life, a good breeder will always offer to have the puppy back should the unforeseeable happen. This should be ascertained from the very outset. Personally, when selling a puppy, I always give a letter confirming the puppy's identity and stating that I am prepared to take the dog back at any stage of his life. I ask the

owner to counter sign, agreeing to this arrangement should ever the unfortunate occasion arise.

It is generally accepted that if, on your first visit to view a litter, you decide to purchase a puppy, a deposit is handed over and the balance paid when you go along to collect. Obviously you must also find out what vaccinations are or are not included in the fee, and whether breeding restrictions apply. Some breeders place restrictions on the puppies they sell and these will be detailed in the Kennel Club documentation received. Such restrictions should be discussed fully beforehand. The most common are that a bitch cannot be bred from and that a male cannot be used at

QUESTIONS TO ASK

You will have questions to ask when you make initial telephone enquiries to a breeder and, doubtless, more will arise if and when you decide to visit the litter. But before taking the decision to travel to meet the breeder, you should ascertain that this is a likely litter from which you wish to choose a puppy, so check out the following:

- Is the litter Kennel Club registered?
- Have the sire and dam been tested for progressive retinal atrophy (PRA)? If so, you must also ask to see the certificates when you visit.
- Are the parents show dogs or pets?
- What breeding are the puppies and what lines do they carry? Ask if both parents will be available to see, or, if the sire is owned by someone else, find out if a photo will be available or whether one can be viewed online.
- If the parents are show dogs, what major awards have they won?
- How many puppies were born in the litter, and how many are still available for sale?
- What sex are the puppies that are available?
- What colours are available?
- How old are the pups now, and when would they be ready to leave?
- Has the litter been raised in the home, or in a kennel?
- Have they been well socialised, and have they yet met any children?
- Will the puppies have been fully or partially vaccinated before they leave, and will this be included in the price?
- Will puppies be microchipped?
- Will any restrictions have been placed on their Kennel Club registrations?
- What is the price?
- Will the breeder continue to offer advice throughout your dog's life and take the Shih Tzu back should unforeseen circumstances arise?

stud, but these restrictions can be lifted at a later stage with the breeder's consent if the Shih Tzu has grown up to be of sufficient quality to procreate.

CHOOSING AN OLDER DOG

Although the benefits of buying a young Shih Tzu puppy are manyfold, there may be a situation where an owner prefers a slightly older dog. It could be that the demands of a boisterous young puppy are a little too much, or perhaps they would like to give a good home to a Shih Tzu who has, for whatever reason, fallen on hard times and needs a new home.

There are several reasons why older dogs are occasionally available, and you must be as certain as you can be why the dog is being offered for re-sale. You should also bear in mind that if you are looking for a show dog, you are unlikely to find an older dog available for show purposes unless you are willing to pay a very high price. Occasionally, successful winning stock is sold on to a breeder/exhibitor abroad, but the fee paid usually runs into thousands of pounds.

Some breeders like to 'run on' more than one puppy from a litter, with the aim of eventually keeping the better of the two. They may even retain three, to keep their options open. Even so, it is unlikely that the puppies

It may be that an older Shih Tzu will fit in better with your lifestyle.

that are eventually to leave will be very old when they are offered for sale, perhaps six months or so.

As with any breed, a promising show puppy may simply not turn out well enough for the show ring. This can be disheartening for any breeder and unless she can accommodate a 'passenger' and has an especially soft heart, the youngster may be offered for sale to a pet home. It is possible that the price of a slightly older puppy, offered for sale for this reason, will be rather less than that of an eight- to 12-week-old youngster.

If purchasing an older puppy, the chances are that he will be at least partly house-trained. However, bear in mind that when a dog goes to a new home he will not know the 'house rules' and will almost certainly need a little re-training. A bonus is that the

older dog will, hopefully, have been trained to walk on a lead, and the course of vaccinations should be complete.

Another possibility of an older dog coming up for sale is when a breeder decides to part with a bitch that has been used for breeding purposes. It may be that she has suffered an illness at a relatively young age, which has caused her to be spayed so she can no longer produce puppies. It may be that she has had a couple or more litters and the breeder now feels it would be best for her to have a different, loving home where she would receive more attention. It may be that there is another dog, perhaps of another breed, that does not get along well with a particular Shih Tzu, so the unfortunate Shih Tzu is rehomed in order to restore harmony.

RESCUED DOGS

Another way of obtaining an older Shih Tzu, and one that can be highly rewarding, is to take on a rescued dog. A dog can become 'a rescue' for a whole host of reasons, some of them very valid, such as when an owner has either died or had to be taken into a care home where pets are not allowed. There are other cases that are not so valid, such as when a new baby arrives in the household, and the decision is made for the dog to go. This should never be allowed to happen, but sadly it does; this matter should have been carefully considered before a puppy joined the family in the first instance.

There are also occasions when a dog that is rescued has a temperament unsuitable for his former home situation. Most good rescue officers will carefully assess a dog's temperament before rehoming and, if necessary, the dog will be put to sleep if it is thought he cannot not be rehomed safely. There are others, though, that can be suitable for other homes, provided the dog's past history and the potentially new environment are very carefully considered. Temperament problems do not usually arise in Shih Tzu, so when they do, it is often people or circumstances that have brought them about.

FINDING A RESCUED DOG
The best places to locate Shih Tzu that are in need of rehoming are the breed specialist clubs, of which there are several in the UK. Details of how to contact them can be obtained from the Kennel Club. The best route is to get in touch with a club secretary, who can, in turn, put you in touch with the rescue officer. Very occasionally, a Shih Tzu, or perhaps a Shih Tzu crossed with another breed, can also be found in another, larger, rescue organisation, but most purebred members of the breed end up within breed-specific rescue organisations.

What you will be asked to pay for a rescued dog depends on several things. You may just be asked to give a donation, or perhaps to cover the cost of any veterinary treatment the dog has had while in the care of the rescue kennels. People who have had dogs through breed rescue societies are always asked to keep in touch so that a track can be

kept of the Shih Tzu's progress. In breed clubs' newsletters you can sometimes find heartening stories of Shih Tzu that have moved to their new homes, where they have found a bountiful supply of happiness, despite their unfortunate past histories.

YOUR NEW DOG
A Shih Tzu is a very special breed, sometimes called a 'little lion' because he is a small dog with a huge heart and an even bigger personality. If you have done your homework well, you will recognise his special needs, particularly in relation to grooming, and you may have decided that this is truly the breed for you. If you have, I can assure you that you have made a wonderful choice!

Taking on a Shih Tzu is a big responsibility – but it is a decision you will never regret.

THE NEW ARRIVAL

Chapter 4

Some days you must have wondered when the long-awaited day of your new puppy's arrival would ever come. But soon enough the big day will arrive and will be the cause of great excitement. You will have been planning for weeks, probably months, and hopefully you will have everything in place for the arrival of your Shih Tzu. Most probably you will be bringing a puppy home, but it could be an older dog; whichever the case, the tension will be immense. Try to stay calm and collected, and, hopefully, your own calmness will rub off on the other members of the family, for this will be infinitely better for your new four-legged charge.

It is vital to start as you mean to go on, and the safety of your Shih Tzu must always be uppermost in your mind. When he first arrives home everything will be unfamiliar to him and he will have no idea where he is, so take care that accidents do not happen. Now is the time he might escape and get lost if you do not keep a very careful eye on him. When he is comfortable with you and settled in your home, things will be different.

GARDEN SAFETY

Your garden must be ultra-safe. A Shih Tzu is only a small dog, so can easily locate the tiniest nook or cranny and use this as a means of escape. Because of the Shih Tzu's coat and large, round eyes, you will also need to be sure there are no sharp thorns around the garden at his level. If you have rose-beds, it would be wise to cordon them off so that he cannot become entangled in them and possibly do damage to his eyes in the process.

Pay particular attention to your garden's boundaries. By no means all Shih Tzu can climb, but there are a few who can, so do keep this in mind. The Shih Tzu is an inquisitive little dog who has a canny capacity for working out how to do things. The garden gate should be very secure, and every member of the family should have strict instructions that it should always be firmly closed. A notice on the gate, asking visitors to close it, is also a very sensible idea. To be on the safe side, you may consider erecting a second, small gate as a means of security. I have an extra three foot (one-metre) gate at the side of the house, so that if tradesmen are allowed through the side gate, the dogs cannot rush up to them and through to the wide, wide world outside.

If you have an ornamental iron gate, you may well need to change this, or line it with something through which a small Shih Tzu cannot wriggle,

especially when just a puppy. A Shih Tzu's coat can make him look deceptively larger than he is, but if you flatten the coat down and measure across the widest point of his ribcage, you will know whether or not you need to make adjustments to your garden. If you have to put up an additional protective covering on your gate, do not use something as fine as 'chicken wire', as your Shih Tzu's teeth could get caught, with disastrous results. Also, take care that no coverings have sharp edges that could damage the coat or the eyes.

When assessing your garden, you should also consider any places that are unsafe, such as terracing from which your Shih Tzu could jump down from a

Patrol the boundaries of your garden to check the fencing – an inquisitive Shih Tzu will attempt to squeeze through the smallest of gaps.

TOILETING AREA

When your new Shih Tzu arrives, he will have no idea where he is expected to do his toilet, so you will need to teach him. If you have young children, it is a sensible idea to designate an area of your garden that your puppy can be trained to use by simply leading him to this every time he goes outside for this purpose. Soon enough he will become accustomed to this area and will, hopefully, use it regularly of his own accord when he grows up.

All faeces must be picked up and disposed of as quickly as possible, for if left lying around, they can become a potential health hazard,

and, in warmer months of the year, will attract flies. If your Shih Tzu has been taught to eliminate on a hard surface, rather than on the grass, this will be easier to hose down and keep ultra-clean.

Copography (eating of faeces) is not common among Shih Tzu, who, after all, seem to have been destined for a diet of curlews' livers and breasts of quail in China, but I am sure there must be a few out there who do have this very unpleasant habit. However, this is all the more reason why you should keep your dog's toilet area clean.

considerable height. Something that may not look particularly dangerous to us as humans would be a mammoth leap for a small dog, and if a dog lands heavily on his lower jaw, as one of mine has done, tooth loss can be the dreaded result.

SAFETY IN THE HOME
Your home should be a place of comfort and security for your Shih Tzu puppy, but it can be a place of danger, too. Some hazards for a puppy may be obvious, but there are other hidden dangers, so it is always better to be safe than sorry.

Anything that is dangerous for a dog, especially for a young puppy, should be kept sufficiently high up and therefore out of reach. Bear in mind, an inquisitive Shih Tzu's nose will go to any lengths to reach an enticing smell, so make sure that all routes to reach dangerous items are also secure. Chocolate, for example, is dangerous for dogs to eat, so do not make the mistake of leaving a tempting open box on your coffee table when you leave the room – not even for a moment.

Because a Shih Tzu is fairly low to the ground, he can squeeze into places larger dogs cannot reach, occasionally giving the game away by leaving clumps of hair that have become attached to things *en route*. Therefore, check everything at ground floor level that is easily accessible. However laborious the task may be, you need to check every room in the house, and if it means going down on all fours yourself, so be it!

The most obviously dangerous items are electric cables, many of which are at floor level, behind the TV, computer system and such like. Many a puppy has secretly nibbled away at the casings around wires, sometimes for days, until eventually the electric cable is reached and the consequences can be fatal.

Obviously all chemicals should be kept out of a puppy's reach, as should household cleaning items; many contain ingredients that can be very harmful if eaten, or sometimes if only touched with the tongue. Pesticides are a real threat, especially slug, mouse

Look at the world from your puppy's perspective so you can spot all possible hazards.

HO ME GROWN

and rat poisons, which can cause serious harm, often not noticed until bleeding occurs, possibly from the dog's gums. If your Shih Tzu appears to have been taken ill due to poisoning, it will help your vet enormously if you take along the box or bottle you believe to have caused the illness, as different poisons often have to be treated in different ways. Quick thinking on your part could save your Shih Tzu's life.

Remember, too, that many foods you generally keep in your kitchen cupboards can be harmful to dogs. Not only chocolate, but also cocoa powder can be a killer if eaten in large quantities; and, unfortunately, dogs do seem to particularly like the taste of chocolate-flavoured products. Raisins and grapes are also especially harmful, so if you drop one or two in error, be sure to pick them up with great speed, before your dog does! Take care about leaving nuts around too, especially macadamia.

Young children must be taught to keep all their playthings tidy, for the puppy's safety. Not only can a puppy's teeth cause enormous damage to a much-loved toy, a toy can also harm a puppy, possibly causing him to choke. Some children's toys, such as Lego, can be particularly unsafe, as the small pieces are just the right size to get stuck in a puppy's throat.

Remember, nothing is safe when a new puppy arrives in your home.

Another great danger – not immediately evident – is glue. Very sadly, a puppy I once sold died while still only a few months old because he had eaten glue used to repair a bicycle wheel. Many children also have games consoles, the wires of which can be very tempting for any puppy, and more often than not the early signs of nibbling go unnoticed until it is too late.

Stairs are another danger for puppies, as are railings, though which a small puppy might fall. A Shih Tzu's coat is abundant, so do not be deceived by the width of the aperture through which he can wriggle, or perhaps run at full pelt while playing. Measure your puppy as described earlier, and make sure that the railings are significantly narrower. If not, you must erect some protection, if only as a temporary measure until your dog matures. Many a time an owner has had to dismantle

railings because a Shih Tzu puppy has managed to get his head through and subsequently become wedged.

Apart from the obvious danger of a puppy falling down the stairs and doing himself damage, you should always keep in mind that a Shih Tzu is a relatively long-bodied dog, so stairs are not so easy for him to negotiate as they might be for other breeds. Some Shih Tzu manage to get up the stairs without problem, but then can never sort out how to get down again.

A wise precaution is to erect a baby gate or, better still, a dog gate; the latter is usually available from dog shows or via the internet. The gate can be set up at the bottom of the stairs if you wish your puppy or your adult dog to be restricted to the ground floor – or you may decide to have one gate at the top and one at the bottom. These are not permanent fixtures and can always be removed once you are confident that your Shih Tzu will come to no harm on the stairs. Afterwards these baby or dog gates can come in very handy if fitted across a doorway, to keep your dog in, or out, of the kitchen, for example. This will keep him safe while you are carrying hot dishes into the dining room. When carrying something it is not always easy to see a small dog in front of you, so there is the danger of tripping over him.

Spend some time reassuring your puppy when you first Introduce him to a crate.

If you feed your puppy in his crate, it helps to build up positive associations.

BUYING EQUIPMENT

It is important to ensure that everything is ready for the homecoming to make your puppy's transition from one home to the next as smooth as possible.

CRATE

Personally, although I have crates, my dogs use them rarely, primarily just for travelling and when they are at shows. But their uses are manyfold and quite a lot of owners like their Shih Tzu to sleep in crates, depending on the set-up at home.

Certainly a new puppy should be crate trained, for there are always times when a crate comes in useful. If he were to visit the vet's for an operation he would be crated there, so if he is already familiar with using one, this will make his time in the veterinary surgery far less stressful. If you enter your Shih Tzu for a Championship Dog Show, he has to be crated while at the show, and it is always safer for a dog to travel in a crate for a car journey, rather than to sit on the seat. Should you, unfortunately, be involved in a traffic accident, your dog will stand a much better chance of coming off unscathed if he is confined to a crate – and there will be less chance of distracting the driver if a puppy is not jumping around the seats.

When first introduced to a crate, a puppy may not take easily to the idea, but if properly trained, he will soon get used to it and come to consider it his own special place. It is always a good idea to confine a puppy to a crate for very short periods while you are in the house, so you can keep an eye on him. Then, when the time comes that you genuinely need to leave him in a crate, you will feel secure in your mind that he will be happy if shut in for a while.

Many people who do not have dogs, and indeed many who do, are not at all fond of crates, but crates are not cages, and if you leave the crate door open with a comfortable bed inside, and perhaps a toy, you will often find your Shih Tzu goes in there of his own free will. When I had to fly my dogs abroad with me, I know their journey was much easier for

IDENTIFICATION

In Britain it is a legal requirement for all dogs to carry a visible form of identification when in a public place, so even if you have your Shih Tzu microchipped, he will still need a tag around his neck, giving contact details should he get lost.

In America dog laws vary between states, so you will need to check what the requirements are in your area.

Tags come in two types: those that are engraved, often available from shoe-repair shops, and those on which details are hand-written and contained in a tiny barrel attached to the dog's collar. The latter must be checked on a daily basis to be sure the bottom of the barrel has not come undone and fallen off. Always keep spares in stock. Because of the length of an adult Shih Tzu's coat, you must also check regularly that hair has not become entangled in the fastening.

In addition to the wearing of a tag attached to the collar, some people have their Shih Tzu microchipped, or have the ears tattooed. I personally consider the former preferable. The microchip that is inserted between the shoulder blades is the size of a grain of rice, but I have only ever had one of my own dogs flinch when it was inserted, and that was only for a fleeting moment. If a dog is travelling abroad, microchipping is essential.

them because of their familiarity with a crate. They just assumed they were off to another show, instead of travelling halfway around the world!

You may decide to have one crate for inside the home and another for travel. This will save you the effort of humping the crate in and out of the car, even though most are collapsible. Select your crate/s carefully though. Each must be must be sufficiently large for your dog to stand up in, and big enough in which to turn around and lie down comfortably – 18 ins x 24 ins (46 x 61 cms) is probably best, but you could get away with one slightly smaller if yours is a small Shih Tzu. If you have two dogs that get along well together,

you may decide to have a larger crate that will accommodate both of them.

Crates come in varying qualities, and the more expensive ones can last for many a long year, so you are probably better forking out a little more money to get the best crate from the start. Check, too, that the safety catch is a good one; this fixture can be lacking in some of the cheaper models. Some crates have doors on both the short and long sides; these can be useful if you know you will need to position your crate in different places.

Inside the crate you should line the base with newspaper, and then add veterinary bedding, which is easy to wash and must always be kept scrupulously

clean. If you have difficulty obtaining this type of bedding at a pet store, you are sure to find it at any of the larger Championship shows. It comes in large sheets so you can cut it to size and have spare pieces available when one is being washed.

You will also need a water bowl suitable for a crate. I find the best type is the one that hooks on to the side of the crate, but non-spill bowls are also available for travelling. Some owners prefer to use 'rabbit feeders', but not all dogs take easily to these.

As your Shih Tzu reaches maturity and knows all the rules of the house, you may decide to dispense with a crate inside the home and replace it with a dog bed. But your dog must always have a place to call his own. I would, however, urge you still to use a crate when travelling in the car.

FEEDING BOWLS

Stainless-steel feeding bowls are undoubtedly the most hygienic; not only can they be easily washed, but there is no chance of them becoming cracked or chipped and thereby harbouring germs. Stainless-steel bowls are readily available from pet stores and major retail outlets. The second choice would be ceramic bowls; some owners prefer to use these for water, as they are heavier and less likely to spill, but avoid plastic bowls at all costs, as they can be very easily be chewed, particularly by sharp puppy teeth.

COLLAR AND LEAD

When your Shih Tzu puppy first comes home, he will need a secure collar and lead of suitable size, which will not be too heavy for him. Check that the catch is secure, both on the collar and at the end of the lead. Most collars are adjustable, but be careful not to make the collar so loose that it can slip over the puppy's head if, for example, he decides to pull in the opposite direction (as he is likely to do if he becomes scared). On the other hand, the collar should never be too tight; check that you can slide one or two fingers beneath it.

As your puppy grows, you will need to get a larger collar and a more substantial lead. The choice

There is a huge choice of collars and leads, but to begin with, concentrate on buying a secure collar and a lightweight lead.

is vast, but if you plan to keep your Shih Tzu in long coat, do not select a rolled, leather collar, as the coat will get twisted around it.

If you plan to show your Shih Tzu, you will also need one or more show leads; most of us have a bag full, although there is always one special favourite. There are various slightly different types of show lead, and you may need to experiment with two or three of these before deciding which suits you best. Having the

right lead in the show ring can make the difference between the dog giving a good performance on the move and a bad one. Ultimately this may mean the difference between wining a first prize and winning no award at all.

GROOMING EQUIPMENT

Because you have chosen a heavily coated breed, grooming equipment will require some investment. While your puppy is still young, you will be able to get away with a high-quality brush, a steel-toothed comb, and a pair of nail clippers. Some Shih Tzu owners also use a slicker brush, but for a puppy this must be as soft as possible. Even for adult dogs, the brush should never be of the hardest variety.

Grooming will be an essential part of daily care for your Shih Tzu, whether he is kept in long coat or in pet trim, so you should have the basic grooming tools ready and waiting for the day that you bring your puppy home. As soon as he has settled in, perhaps on the second or third day, mini-grooming sessions should commence. Hopefully, he will have come to you looking spick and span, but although you may think he does not need to be groomed yet, you must get him used to the routine.

It is also a good idea to get him used to having his teeth cleaned from a young age, so I suggest you invest in some doggy toothpaste and a child's toothbrush. A puppy's teeth do not really need cleaning, but you

If you plan to keep your Shih Tzu in full coat, you will have to invest in a top-quality grooming kit

should start as you mean to go on and get him into practice while your pup is still young.

As your puppy grows older, you will need to increase the amount of grooming equipment you have for him, and I know you will feel very proud when his head-fall is long enough to tie up in elastic on the top of his head; you are sure to think him the sweetest Shih Tzu you have ever seen! I would suggest you try to get these bands early, as they are not easily available, other than from shows. The usual elastic bands are far too large; what you will need are 'dental elastics'. Remember, you must never pull them out or you will break the coat; they should be cut out carefully with scissors each time they are changed.

For more information on grooming, see Chapter Five: The Best of Care.

TOYS AND TREATS

Most Shih Tzu like to play with toys, but there are exceptions. Some seem to get more pleasure out of a sock they have surreptitiously dragged out of the bathroom than they do from a whole box-full of toys. Others have one favourite toy of all time, while there are also those that enjoy a wide selection.

When choosing toys for your new Shih Tzu puppy, make sure they are not too large – but not small enough to swallow. They should not be too heavy or your puppy will not be able to carry them around, nor should they be of the kind to be tugged on. Always remember that Shih Tzu's teeth are very different from the norm and you should allow them to develop naturally. Never tug at a toy in a Shih Tzu's mouth, especially while he is still a puppy, or you can easily bring

the teeth out of alignment.

Check toys regularly to see that no parts have come loose or detached, because these can be very dangerous, especially the squeaky parts inside. Toys that start to look dubious in terms of safety should be discretely removed and thrown away. Bear in mind that if the stuffing comes detached that, too, can be very dangerous, both for a puppy and for an adult dog.

Chew sticks are enjoyed by puppies, but they can become sticky when moist and cause havoc with a Shih Tzu's coat. Pigs' ears also seem to be very popular, but can get smelly when a dog has been chewing at them for a few days. In all cases, when a chew starts to become small enough to swallow and, certainly, if it develops any sharp edges, remove it immediately and replace with a more robust alternative.

FOOD

Before collecting your puppy, the breeder should give you precise instructions about his current feeding regime. This will enable you to purchase a supply of exactly the same brand of food so that there will be as little disruption as possible to his diet. The diet can be changed over the coming weeks, but this must be done gradually, carefully blending the two and gradually increasing the amount of the new food so as to avoid an upset tummy.

It is not unusual for breeders to provide sufficient food to feed a puppy for a few days after his arrival in his new home, but this should be clarified beforehand so you don't find yourself in the difficult situation of not being able to purchase the right kind of food at short notice. A few breeders are also agents who sell food, in which case you will easily be able to purchase a large bag of food from the breeder, until you find a local supplier.

A change of water can also cause tummy trouble, especially if your puppy has travelled from a part of the country where the water is different. It is therefore sensible to use mineral water for the first few days, and to introduce your own tap water slowly. An alternative is to boil the tap water and let it cool before offering it to your dog.

POO BAGS

In many countries, the law obliges you to clean up after your dog, with strict penalties imposed if you fail to do so. Added to this, there is the simple matter of hygiene and surely none of us wants to further aggravate the anti-dog lobby, which will look for any excuse to complain about dogs and their owners.

'Poo' bags are inexpensive and can be purchased from many pet stores. A cheaper alternative is to buy nappy bags from a chemist or supermarket. You can even recycle carrier bags, provided there are no holes in the bottom! At the other end of the scale, it is possible to buy a special dog bag, designed to incorporate a receptacle for poo bags, and a

hygienic container in which to keep the used ones until they can be disposed of.

FINDING A VET

If you have bought your Shih Tzu from a breeder close to home, you can ask which vet they use, and register with the same one, which will be an added bonus for there will be continuity. If this is not the case, the breeder may be able to recommend a practice close to you, or put you in touch with someone who can give you first-hand advice.

If the breeder is not in a position to help, make careful enquiries about the vets in your own area, seeking personal recommendation if possible. In a city, most vets are familiar primarily with small animals, but, in a rural practice, many have more experience with large farm animals than they do with dogs. It is a 'small animal vet' that you will need, or at least one who deals with both.

Some vets do not understand a Shih Tzu's jaw formation, so do not be put off by a vet who tells you that your puppy has an incorrect bite. If your vet does not seem to understand why your Shih Tzu's bite is as it is, change your vet and select another who has done more homework and has more exposure as a small animal practitioner.

A few vets incorporate homoeopathy with traditional veterinary medicine, so if this is available, it may be a suitable option, though it is a matter for personal preference.

It is always wise to visit a surgery before making your first appointment; this will serve to give you a feel for the place and you can assess its cleanliness and the friendliness of the staff, for you will always want your Shih Tzu to be put at his ease when visiting. Also check what the surgery times are and whether it is an appointment system or a 'first come first served' basis,

Your puppy will love to play with toys – but you must ensure they are 100 per cent safe.

Ideally, you want to find a vet who is experienced in treating Shih Tzu.

which can frequently necessitate a long wait.

Check what happens in an emergency or if you need a vet outside normal opening hours. A practice that can respond quickly and efficiently can mean the difference between life and death in a dire emergency. Of course, you hope this will never happen, but it is better to be safe than sorry.

The first occasion you visit your vet will probably be for a routine vaccination, as, depending on your puppy's age upon collection, his course of vaccinations may not be complete. At this time the vet will also check his general health. The breeder will have provided you with full details of vaccinations to date, including a record card, and you will need to hand this to

your vet so that he knows exactly what drugs have been administered and when.

You should also have been provided with details of the puppy's worming programme. This, too, should be discussed with your vet so that he can prescribe whatever he considers suitable for continuation, with details of timing. Worming products prescribed by a vet are much more efficient than those available over the counter.

A Shih Tzu puppy will need to be bathed frequently, so, hopefully, fleas will never be a problem. However, they can be picked up occasionally from other dogs with whom they have come into contact, even if yours is spotlessly clean, so do not be ashamed of this. 'Spot on' treatments are available from your vet and last for several weeks. The small amount of liquid is applied behind the dog's neck, so it cannot be licked, and this is absorbed into the skin. It could be wise to purchase a small quantity of this just to keep in your cupboard at home.

For more information on parasites: see Chapter Eight: Happy and Healthy.

Lastly, if you have decided to have your Shih Tzu microchipped, various people offer this service, but I would recommend you have it done by your vet, though certainly not on a puppy's first visit.

COLLECTING YOUR PUPPY

If possible, make arrangements to collect your puppy fairly early in the day, especially if you have a long journey home ahead of you. This will give you as much time as possible with your puppy to help him settle before bedtime.

Go prepared, armed with plenty of paper towels, damp cloths and dry towels, as some Shih Tzu puppies do not travel well at first. Most soon get used to it, but may dribble a lot or even be sick, especially if the car

SHOPPING LIST

To make sure you are properly prepared for your puppy's arrival, tick off the following items on the list below, at least a couple of days or so before he joins you:

- Crate
- Bed and bedding
- Feeding and water bowls
- Water bowl for travel
- Collar and lead

- Toys and/or treats
- Basic grooming equipment
- Food as advised by the breeder
- Poo bags

At long last it is time to collect your Shih Tzu puppy.

journey is on twisty roads. If you have a choice of routes homeward bound, I would suggest you take the straighter one, even if it puts a few more miles on the journey. It is also likely that your puppy cannot be put down in public places if his course of vaccinations is not complete, so if his journey is long, you will have to make some provision for an opportunity for him to relieve himself; bring plenty of clean newspaper.

A small water bowl is also an essential for the journey, with a bottle of mineral water or boiled tap water that has been left to cool. Your puppy may refuse a drink on the way home, but it must be available, especially in hot weather.

If the breeder is thoughtful, you may be given a small piece of bedding from the whelping box, which will help your little puppy to feel more secure on his journey. In any event you should bring something that will be comfortable for him to lie on.

If you are using a crate in the car, rather than putting your puppy alone in the back of the car, place the crate on one of the collapsible seats in the rear and recruit someone to sit on the adjacent seat to give him reassurance and to check he is not being sick. Make sure a drink of water is always at the ready, as he may become very thirsty if stressed and you must not allow him to dehydrate.

MEETING THE FAMILY

Your Shih Tzu is almost certain to have an outgoing personality, but arriving in a new home will be overwhelming for him, so, initially, keep introductions to the close members of your family. Of course, everyone will want to meet the new youngster that has just joined your life. But the puppy needs to get to know those who will become the closest to him, otherwise he will not only become even more overwhelmed, but increasingly confused. He needs to get to know the people who will look after him all the time so that his faith in them can grow, and, with it, respect for his new family circle.

Explain to all those people who

PAPERWORK

Although your entire attention is sure to revolve around your new Shih Tzu puppy, make sure you are given the important documentation that the breeder should have ready for you. You should be given the following:
- Kennel Club registration certificate
- Pedigree (ideally five generations)
- Receipt
- Feeding plan
- A list of medications so far administered, including details of the worming regime that should already have been commenced.

- Contract. The breeder may also have asked you to sign a statement confirming that if ever you are unable to keep the Shih Tzu, he will be returned to the breeder.
- Insurance. The breeder may provide free insurance for the first few weeks of the puppy's time with you. It will then be up to you whether you decide to continue to insure with this provider, or change to another company. Of course, you may decide not to take out insurance for the future, but it would be advisable to do so.

are anxious to meet your puppy that in fairness to him, you want to give him a settling-in period, so that he can develop into a well-adjusted Shih Tzu adult.

Always bear in mind that this is the first time your puppy will have left his siblings and also his mother, so he will feel very much alone. Carry him into the house calmly and without appearing to be over-excited. If there are children at home waiting for the puppy's arrival, you should have instructed them beforehand that they should be waiting as quietly as possible, sitting down, preferably on the floor, rather than running around. A puppy is very small, so he is likely to feel intimidated by large human beings towering above him, especially if they are rushing around from place to place.

But before meeting the children, the first port of call will be puppy's toilet area; he may have had a long journey and is probably desperate to relieve himself. Then show him his crate or sleeping quarters and only then introduce him to the children who, as the days and weeks progress, are sure to become an integral part of his life.

Do not allow young children to pick up the puppy at this early stage. Just encourage them to stroke him gently, always approaching from under the chin rather than from above the head. After the initial introductions are over, you may well find that your puppy has settled down sufficiently to want to explore his surroundings, but only allow him to investigate those areas in the close vicinity. He will need to become familiar with just one or two areas at a time. If you have a large garden, you should probably wait several days before you allow him the free run of the entire area.

Little by little, over the coming days, you will be able to introduce him to your wider circle of family and friends, and, when his course of vaccinations is complete, you will be able to introduce him to other dogs, too.

Socialisation at a young age will be an essential part of your puppy's mental development, allowing him to become a well-adjusted companion.

PETS WELCOME

Your puppy will need to be introduced slowly and carefully to the other pets in your household, always under close supervision. It is unlikely that your puppy will take an aversion to them, but they may decide they are not so fond of him.

It will not be long before your puppy becomes established in the family.

If you supervise early interactions, your resident dog will soon accept the new arrival.

A Shih Tzu and a cat will learn to live in harmony – but it may take a bit of time...

If you already have an older dog, it is likely that the Shih Tzu puppy will be submissive, and usually the older of the two will realise he is only a youngster and will be gentle with him. But this does not mean you should not always be on your guard, and never leave them alone together until you feel certain that their relationship is stable.

It is always wise to introduce dogs on neutral territory. Do not, for example, let the puppy go bounding up to your older dog on his bed, which he will probably guard; this will not bode well for their future relationship. Never ignore your older dog in favour of the puppy; you should, when possible, greet the older dog first, followed by the youngster. In time they will sort out their own pecking order.

Mealtimes can be a source of tension. Never feed both dogs from the same dish, and dishes should be kept well apart when meals are served. You need to know exactly what the young puppy is eating – and you do not want his food gulped down by a greedy adult! If you are not aware of how much your puppy is eating, you will wonder why he is losing weight.

Likewise, beds should be kept apart, and obviously each dog should have his own base. In time they may happily snuggle up together in the same bed, but they must each have the opportunity to have their private space when they want it. If your older dog has his own special toy, make sure you have bought another toy for the puppy, as the older dog may become possessive if the youngster tries to steal his 'treasure'. Again, in time, they will probably share their toys freely, but avoid any unnecessary aggravation from the outset.

Introducing the family cat can be a different matter. I have always found that cats keep their distance from the newcomer for a few days, without either party being restricted. However, other owners feel it best to crate the puppy and let the cat into the room to sniff around, before letting the puppy out on a lead. Most Shih Tzu take to lead training fairly easily, so this strategy may be worth trying. However, you will need to take care that the cat does not lash out at your puppy's eyes.

Introducing a Shih Tzu to smaller pets is not usually a problem, as, more often than not, a rabbit, hamster, mouse or pet rat has his own cage. I have found that rabbits who have freedom around house and garden have always got along well with small dogs, as long as they are not terriers – and with sighthounds it is quite a different matter!

Arriving in a new home is a daunting experience for a puppy.

THE FIRST NIGHT

The very last duty you have to your new puppy before settling him down for the night in his new home is to let him out to his toilet area. Even if he does not seem to want to relieve himself, give him time and, hopefully, he will. This will make for a much more comfortable start to the long, lonely hours of darkness.

Because your puppy will be unfamiliar with his surroundings and will miss his mother and his siblings, you should put something safe into his crate or sleeping quarters so that he can cuddle up, albeit to an inanimate object, such as a cuddly toy.

There is every chance that he will cry when he realises he has been left alone, and the temptation will be for you to go back to him to calm him down. This may not be the best solution; you would be better advised to leave him to cry for a while and he should calm down of his own accord, at which time you can creep quietly off to bed, in preparation for an early rise!

However, if your puppy gets really distraught, you will have to go in again to settle him down and allay his fears – being alone for the first time in his life cannot be much fun. His distress will probably have tired him out, so if you are soft-hearted, like me, you will probably decide to stay with him until he falls into a deep sleep, at which time you can once more creep away as silently as a mouse!

HOUSE RULES

Just as with a child, when your Shih Tzu puppy joins your household he will have to learn what is, and what is not, expected of him. His mealtimes should be set at regular intervals but, depending on his age, these will probably be reduced in number as he matures. He should have been introduced to his toilet area and although mistakes are sure to happen in the early days, at least the rules will have been set.

If you do not wish your puppy to get on the bed or other furniture, you must make this clear to him from the outset. It is absolutely no good picking him up to sit with you on one occasion, and telling him to get off the sofa on another. You should also bear in mind that a Shih Tzu, being a relatively short-legged, long-bodied breed, should not be allowed to jump up and down from heights that, in relation to his size, are enormous. This can cause him great damage, including back injury, and can cause his bone structure to develop incorrectly.

Consistency is of great importance, for if your puppy is allowed to do something on one occasion and not the next, he will be a very confused little individual.

House rules do not only apply to your new puppy, but to your family as well. Small children must be taught never to tug at the coat, which, as it grows, may be very tempting. Do not allow children to feed titbits to your puppy for what seems like a very tasty treat to your child may be totally unsuitable for a dog.

Another highly important house rule is that doors and gates should be closed at all times; there would be nothing worse than your precious new friend escaping, and just think how badly the offender would feel, too.

HOUSE-TRAINING

A puppy needs to pee and poo much more often than an adult dog, and when he wakes up, he simply cannot wait. If he is not already awake, the chances are that he will be up on his feet and ready for the day ahead when he hears the household stir, so don't wait to get dressed or put the kettle on, let him out straight away before he has time to have an accident.

A puppy will need to relieve himself very often – about every one or two hours and especially after eating and sleeping. This frequency will reduce

substantially as he grows up, but, until then, you will need to be vigilant and watch for every sign. Until he knows that he must ask at the door, the first sign will be sniffing the ground, and then probably turning around in a circle, at which time you must pick him up immediately and take him to his toilet area or, when he is a little older, open the door quickly and indicate that he must go out.

Never chastise your puppy unless you actually catch him in the act of doing his toilet in the wrong place. If you do, you will only confuse him. He will not connect the two incidents, and will have absolutely no idea why he is being told off. Most Shih Tzu like to be clean around the house, so puppy training is not likely to be a problem, although there is sure to be the occasional accident to start with.

PUPPY EXERCISE

You will need to wait until your puppy's course of vaccinations is complete before you can take him out in public places, but there is no reason why you cannot begin some training in your garden sooner than this. Although most Shih Tzu take to a lead fairly readily, a few do not, so the sooner you can start to give him a little practice, the better.

Get him used to his collar first of all. This can be attached inside the house and you should always stay with him until he is comfortable with it, for he is almost certain to try to scratch it

The key to house training is establishing a routine.

off. Although his hair is not yet very long, it can still get tangled if he scratches.

You will need to wait until your puppy is at least six months old before he is allowed to free run off the lead, and even then only in a very safe place and under close supervision.

For more information on training, see Chapter Six.

TAKING ON AN OLDER DOG

In the same way as a puppy, an older dog may feel very apprehensive when being introduced to his new home; everything will be just as strange for him. His past circumstances will also have a bearing on how easily he can adjust. He may have had an unhappy life, so he may be frightened of things such as doors closing on him, which may indicate to him that he will be shut in for hours on end, or he may be afraid of people's legs if he has been kicked. Yes, sadly it does happen.

On the other hand, he may have enjoyed many happy years living with a devoted owner who has either died or been taken into a care home where dogs are not allowed. In such circumstances he is sure to be missing his owner dreadfully, and you will have to take this into consideration. Indeed, it often takes longer for an older dog to settle into a new home than it does a puppy.

Introduce the older dog to your home much as you would a puppy, and remember that he does not know the house rules either. He may have been perfectly clean around the house in his former home, but now he will not be sure where he should do his toilet. For example, if he is used to grass, and you have none, he may decide your rug is the nearest thing to the texture of grass.

The same rules apply as for a youngster: do not introduce him to all and sundry in one fell swoop. Introduce your family and friends slowly, allowing him to get used to each one individually. Never force yourself on any dog – and do not allow your friends to impose themselves. In his own good time, your new pet will strike up his bond of friendship. But he should decide when this will happen, not you, nor your friends and relations. Be patient!

If you are taking on an older dog, try to find out as much as possible about his background.

FEEDING

Depending on how you came into contact with your new adult friend, you may have been given a diet sheet by the rescue centre or breed rescue representative from whom you collected your dog. It is unlikely that you will have collected the dog from his previous owner, but, if this is the case, be sure to ask what food has been given and whether meals have been provided once or twice a day.

As for a puppy, a change to the diet should be made slowly so as not to upset your Shih Tzu's tummy. Do not worry if he is not over-enthusiastic about food for the first couple of days. He will eat when he is hungry, and probably when you are not looking. Some Shih Tzu prefer to eat alone, and some of them like to take a few small pieces away from their dish to eat in a quiet corner somewhere. If your newly acquired pet has not eaten for two full days after arrival, you should consult your vet, but usually a Shih Tzu can be enticed with a piece of boneless white chicken meat, and, once he has started to eat, hopefully he will never look back. Again, it may be sensible to offer only bottled water or cooled, boiled water for the first few days, then gradually introduce your local tap water.

TRAINING STRATEGY

Although the older Shih Tzu you have taken on may already be well trained, or reasonably so,

You may need to help your Shih Tzu with house training for the first few weeks.

you should be prepared for all eventualities so that unsociable situations, or things of which you do not approve, do not arise.

Because he does not know where he is at first, he may be tempted to bark if left alone outside, so initially you should stay with him to give reassurance. The people who visit your home and even walk past your gate will be different from the people he came across before, so once again reassure him that he has nothing to fear. Do not forget to praise him when he has done something of which you approve.

If he appears overly nervous about something, do not cuddle and cosset him too much or he will pick up on your own vibrations and may feel even more unsure. Instead, try to ignore him, all the while keeping

an eye on him. Then, when he is calm, give him plenty of praise for overcoming his fears.

If house-training your new adult Shih Tzu is a problem at first, do not get angry with him. Soon enough he will learn what he should do, where and when. The Shih Tzu is a breed that likes to be clean and your new-found friend will be as happy as you are when his toileting routine is finally sorted out.

EXERCISE

A newly acquired older Shih Tzu should be treated in much the same way as a youngster, in that you should introduce him slowly to new situations and walks in different areas. The busiest areas should always be left until last. Until you are absolutely certain that he is confident with you and has accepted you as his new owner, he should not be let off the lead. Until then, there is always a chance that he will run off and try to find his way back to his original home for he will have no idea how far away from his first home he has moved.

LIVING WITH CHILDREN

Whether or not your Shih Tzu puppy or adult gets along easily with children will depend very largely upon whether he has been raised in a family with children. To a small child, a Shih Tzu can look very much like a furry toy – but this is exactly what he is not.

A Shih Tzu's coat is always a temptation for a child, but tugging at a coat hurts. The Shih Tzu is a highly tolerant breed, but apart from the obvious damage to the coat itself, it could result in the dog snapping at the child. This would be the case for any breed, not just the Shih Tzu. It is therefore imperative that children are introduced to dogs very carefully and are taught exactly what is, and what is not, acceptable when fondling a new pet.

Children should never be left alone with a dog, at least not until you are absolutely confident that they get along well together and that no harm is likely to come to either party.

After a few weeks it may be possible for an older, sensible child to take your dog out for a walk in a secure place. This should most certainly not be attempted until everyone is absolutely confident that the dog is happy to walk on a lead and will not be fazed by any situation that is thrown at him.

Should you have any queries about how well your older Shih Tzu is adjusting in his new home, if you have obtained him from a rescue society, there should always be someone who is ready to speak to you on the telephone, at least to help you through the first few weeks that are so important in establishing a good relationship for the future.

It is always sad if a dog is not able to stay with his original owner, for whatever reason, but whatever circumstances have befallen your Shih Tzu in the past, hopefully you will be able to redress that by the love and attention you will give him until the very end of his days.

It is very rewarding to give an older dog the chance of finding a home for life.

THE BEST OF CARE

Chapter 5

The general health and condition of a dog starts with a good-quality, well-balanced diet. The breeder will have started the process long before the puppies are born by feeding the mother a nutritious diet. The mother will continue the process when the puppies are born. The breeder then takes over at weaning and continues providing a diet suitable for the puppies' needs until it is time for them to go to their new homes. From then on, it is the new owner's responsibility, which will continue for the duration of the dog's life.

CHOOSING A DIET

Possibly one of the most important decisions you will make regarding the care of your Shih Tzu is what kind of food you are going to feed; whether it is a complete dry food, conventional wet food with biscuit, or the BARF diet (Biologically Appropriate Raw Food, also known as Bone and Raw Food). There are such wide ranges of products available now that it can become very confusing. One point that needs to be emphasised is that if you use a prepared diet, whether it be dry complete, tinned complete or wet food and biscuits, you need to be aware that you are reliant on the manufacturer using good-quality and appropriate products. Recommendation and past experience count for more than any advertisement.

If, at any stage during your dog's life, you need to change his diet, do it gradually. Begin the process by mixing three-quarters of the original diet to a quarter of the new diet at each meal. If there is no adverse reaction, the next day progress to half and half. The following day, move on to a quarter of the original diet with three-quarters of the new diet. By the following day, your dog should be ready for a complete changeover to the new diet. This gradual transition should prevent him from having problems with diarrhoea.

WHICH TYPE OF FOOD?

The basic requirements needed in a Shih Tzu's diet protein, carbohydrates, vitamins and minerals.

- **Protein:** This is essential for growth in puppies and maintenance of adults. It can be found in chicken, turkey, beef, lamb, fish and eggs.
- **Carbohydrates:** This is required for energy and comes from rice, pasta, biscuit and potato.
- **Vitamins and minerals:** These help to maintain optimum health in a variety of ways, such as keeping the immune system healthy,

A complete food provides for all your dog's nutritional needs.

Canned food is appetising, but it has a high moisture content.

promoting healthy skin, teeth and bones. It is important to provide the right balance, as oversupplementation can lead to as many problems as deficiency. Minerals and vitamins are found in meat, green vegetables, eggs, cheese, fish and cereals.

COMPLETE FOOD

Over recent years there have been major advances in manufacturing dry complete food. Virtually all manufacturers now produce food for puppies through to veterans (over seven years old), with diets tailored to meet specific needs. Most of these foods have been developed with the help of vets, who have studied the requirements needed through the varying stages of a dog's life. A diet for sensitive stomachs is readily available, as is one for sensitive skins, or a light diet for the potentially overweight dog. There are also veterinarian diets available for the vast majority of canine conditions, although these can only be provided under veterinary supervision.

The biggest advantage of complete food is that it provides the correct levels of protein, carbohydrates, vitamins and minerals that a dog requires, without having to supplement in any way. At least one manufacturer has now developed breed-specific diets, as well as different sized kibble, dependent on the size of the breed. The instructions regarding quantities to feed according to adult weight are easy to follow and are printed on every bag manufactured.

Some manufacturers produce cans, pouches or hermetically sealed tubs of complete food for puppies through to seniors. Again, these provide everything that the dog requires through various stages of his life, without having to add any supplements. Veterinarian diets, which require veterinary supervision, are also available in cans or pouches. The amounts required are clearly printed on the packaging.

OTHER CANNED FOOD

Most canned food available from pet stores or supermarkets is designed to be mixed with biscuit. Most brands have a very high moisture content and, as with most things in life, you usually get what you pay for.

WET FOOD

Tripe, chicken, lamb, beef, and combinations of these, are now easily purchased in frozen packs and are available from the majority of pet shops. These have to be defrosted and then mixed with a good-quality mixer or small-bite mixer. The packaging of the meat gives a rough approximation as to the daily requirements for the size of the dog. Small-bite mixer also gives an approximate daily requirement as well as providing some essential nutrients.

One disadvantage of this diet could be that you do not know the quantities of essential nutrients you are feeding your dog.

THE BARF DIET
(Biologically Appropriate Raw Food – also known as Bones and Raw Food)
The BARF diet is based on the theory that a dog would eat the whole carcass of a dead animal in the wild, and from this would obtain a balanced diet. The pioneer vet, Dr Ian Billingshurst, who champions this form of feeding, has written a number of books on this subject, including *Give Your Dog a Bone* and *The BARF Diet*, which explain the ethos of the diet.

The basic outline of the diet is to provide a variety of raw foods, with lots of raw, meaty bones (chicken wings, chicken necks, rabbit, oxtail, minced meats, lamb shanks), eggs and their shells, liver, heart, fish, yoghurt, pulped vegetables, garlic and fruit. Information regarding this diet is readily available on the internet.

A gentle warning regarding the BARF diet – introduce your Shih Tzu to raw bones slowly. Dogs have to learn to chew them without choking. Possibly try introducing your dog to a small piece of chicken or turkey neck before progressing to a full wing.

WATER

It is vitally important that your Shih Tzu has access to fresh, clean water at all times; lack of water can soon lead to health problems. Keep the water bowl/container in the same place so your Shih Tzu becomes accustomed to this and knows where to find it. You will soon be able to gauge how much he normally drinks in a day.

A healthy Shih Tzu will not starve himself, therefore he will eat and drink. If he is not hungry, he will not eat, but he will still drink. If he is not eating or drinking, or not eating but drinking excessively, he may be ill, and should be seen by a vet.

FEEDING A PUPPY

Shih Tzu puppies are ready to leave for their new homes at about 10 weeks old and should be having four meals a day: breakfast, lunch, tea and supper. Shih Tzu puppies grow most quickly between the ages of 8 and 20 weeks. Between the ages

of 8 and 10 weeks, they eat the highest proportion of food relative to their body weight. Different lines (families) of Shih Tzu grow at different paces. Some may have finished growing by the time they are five months old, others continue to grow until they are nearly a year old.

A responsible Shih Tzu breeder should provide you with a diet plan for your new puppy. The breeder will have spent many years perfecting the diet they use for their puppies. If you were to speak to six breeders of Shih Tzu, you would probably hear of six different diets fed to puppies. Hopefully, they will explain why they have chosen their preferred diet.

As discussed in Chapter Four, most breeders will give you a few days' supply of food to enable you to feed the same food that your puppy has been used to. This will help him settle in his new surroundings where he is

experiencing many changes. He could be suffering from stress due to leaving his mother and siblings, so he will need plenty of reassurance and encouragement. Some puppies may not eat when they first leave their littermates. This can be because there is no rivalry for the food, or it could even be because of something as simple as a change of feeding bowl. Ask the breeder what kind of dish or plate they have been using. Persevere – this is not the time to give in or to try tempting your puppy with tidbits or other types of food. There is a very real danger that the puppy will quickly accept this as the norm and, worse still, expect a tantalising new treat at every mealtime. Remember, a healthy dog will not starve himself.

It is also helpful if the breeder gives you about a litre of their water. This will enable you to gradually introduce your puppy to his new water, hopefully

A puppy will need four meals a day when he first arrives in his new home.

avoiding the possibility of an upset tummy.

By the time your puppy reaches the age of four months, he should be having three meals a day, and two meals a day by the age of six months. If you are feeding a complete dry food, the suggestion is that you should change to the adult formula at about 10 months of age.

There is a theory that by the time a puppy is four months old, he is half his adult weight, and at six months old he is two-thirds his adult weight. This is a rough guide and not set in stone. As previously said, different Shih Tzu grow at different rates.

In most cases, it is best to feed your Shih Tzu two regular meals a day.

FEEDING REGIMES

When you have decided what type of food you are going to provide, you need to decide what feeding regime will suit you and your Shih Tzu.

REGULAR MEALS

Feeding your Shih Tzu at a regular time will enable him to settle into a routine. If you are feeding your adult Shih Tzu once a day, keep to the same time every day. If you have decided to feed twice a day, try to spread the meals evenly through the day – breakfast in the morning, and a second meal in the early evening. Try not to feed too late in the evening, as this will not give your Shih Tzu time to relieve himself before bedtime.

Never allow your Shih Tzu to be a nuisance when you are eating your own meals, and never feed him tidbits from the table. This is not a good habit and has the potential to lead to obesity in your Shih Tzu. He may also decide that he prefers your food to his.

FREE FEEDING

If you choose this regime you will be providing your Shih Tzu with food 24 hours a day. If you have a greedy dog, he may gorge himself, which is not good for his digestive system and will very probably give him an upset tummy. Free feeders often become lethargic; they lose their enthusiasm for meals. If you use this regime, you will have to use a complete dried food, as wet or canned food would dry out

within a few hours. You also have to bear in mind that as soon as flies appear, they will lay eggs on the food, therefore making a very unhealthy meal for your Shih Tzu. Most vets and breeders do not recommend this regime.

OBESITY

The majority of cases of obesity are the fault of the owners. You must resist giving in to those beautiful Shih Tzu eyes begging you for food when you are eating. It is reckoned that 25 per cent of all dogs seen by vets are overweight; their bodyweight is noticeably more than is normal for their breed. Of these dogs, 25 per cent are obese; the additional fat can be grasped in folds of skin.

Obesity is the most common nutritional problem seen in dogs. The reason for obesity is that the dog has taken in more calories than he needs. The extra calories are converted to fat and are then stored in the body. Being overweight has major health consequences, such as heart disease, diabetes, joint problems leading to arthritis, breathing difficulties, liver function reduction, impairment of digestive function, an increased susceptibility to disease, and shorter life expectancy. An obese dog is unable to walk comfortably and will pant heavily if he is asked to run. He would prefer to sleep rather than play and will have difficulty going up or down steps or slopes.

With a healthy Shih Tzu, you should be able to feel the ribs,

PUPPY CARE

To begin with, accustom your Shih Tzu to being handled so he learns to relax on the grooming table.

Gently brush through the coat.

Now try combing the coat.

Wipe around the eyes and whiskers.

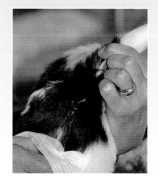

Coat soiling can be a problem, so check and wipe your puppy's bottom on a daily basis.

but you should not be able to see them. He will be bright and alert and ready to play. He will be eager for his food, but not constantly begging for more or pestering you while you are eating.

If you think you may have an obese dog, do not hesitate to seek veterinary advice. You could be killing your dog with kindness.

GROOMING
The grooming process for a Shih Tzu is exactly the same for a puppy as it is for an adult, the difference being the volume and length of coat in an adult. It is worthwhile buying a good-quality pin brush (without knobs on the ends of the pins), as this will see you through into adulthood. Some people prefer a bristle brush, but these can cause static. You will also need a metal comb or two, one with quite wide teeth and another with narrower. Some manufacturers make a comb with a combination of teeth.

PUPPY CARE
Start getting your puppy used to being groomed from a young age.

This will be of benefit when he is older and has a wealth of coat. When you have your puppy on your lap, gently stroke the length of his body with your hand, then progress to the brush and then to the comb. When the pup is relaxed, turn him on to his back and brush his underside, ensuring you do under his front legs and around the inside of his back legs. You can then progress to his chest, neck and around his ears.

While grooming his ears, check that they are not dirty or have dried wax in them. Examine the

PUPPY TOP-KNOT

As your puppy's coat starts to grow, he will need to get used to having his top-knot done.

area just behind his ears carefully; this hair is very soft and mats easily. You should also check that the hairs growing in his ears are not too long; these will need to be gently pulled out.

On a daily basis, clean your puppy's face around his eyes and his whiskers. Then gently groom his head using a brush, then a comb. If you find any knots, do not pull them out with the comb, as this will hurt him and could put him off for life. Gently tease the knot apart with the comb or your fingers until the area can be combed without pulling. Also, try to get the puppy used to you examining his mouth and teeth with a cotton wool bud or with your little finger. This will help

when you want to clean his teeth when he is older and has his adult teeth. There are now different flavoured toothpastes available, which most dogs seem to enjoy.

At certain stages through puppyhood, your Shih Tzu will have tender gums due to teething. At this time you will need to be very gentle around his mouth. Another area that should be checked regularly is his bottom. Coat soiling can be to a major problem, which may necessitate a full bottom wash. There are many products on the market made specifically for cleaning faces, ears and bottoms, as the need arises.

TYING A TOPKNOT
When the hair on a Shih Tzu

head gets longer, it will need to be tied into a topknot. "Not easy!" I can hear you saying – well, you are probably right. This is when ultimate patience is needed. Try to get a straight parting across the bridge of the nose between the eyes. Now brush or comb the hair on the head towards the neck. Using a comb, make a parting above each eye towards the top of the skull. Now make another parting across the top of the skull. You should now have an oblong of hair. Give it a gentle comb, and then use a small elastic band to hold it in place. A topknot should never be too tight, as it will pull on the eyes and destroy the beautiful Shih Tzu expression.

MAKING THE DECISION

The coat of a Shih Tzu puppy is quite easy to maintain until he is about five months old. By this age you will be able to see the adult coat coming through. The coat may become very dense nearest the body; it may also be a slightly different colour. It is at this point that you may decide to have your puppy trimmed. Many owners opt for a pet trim, which, if done well, looks smart and is easy to maintain. In most cases, an adult Shih Tzu will need to be trimmed every 12 to 16 weeks. This can be done by a professional groomer, or your puppy's breeder may be prepared to help.

At around the five month stage, you may find quite a lot of very soft undercoat is coming away in the brush. This is perfectly normal and is the start of his coat maturing. Around the age of nine to ten months, he will start to lose most of his puppy coat. It can be quite daunting, as his coat may look like cotton-wool. To make your life a little bit easier, use a grooming spray to help with removing the shedding hair. Grooming sprays are readily available at pet shops.

Time to decide: Are you going to keep your Shih in full coat or opt for a pet trim?

Full coat.

Pet trim.

An American Champion clipped down after retiring from the show ring.

GROOMING: PET TRIM

Start by brushing through the coat. This Shih Tzu prefers to sit or stand when he is being groomed. Others are happy to lie down.

Now comb through the coat, paying particular attention to the feathering.

The feathering on the ears needs special attention.

ROUTINE CARE FOR PET TRIM AND FULL COAT

Teeth will need to be cleaned on a regular basis.

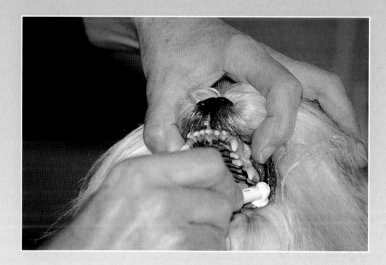

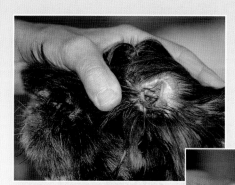

Hair can grow quite profusely within the ears.

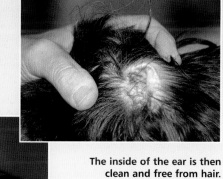

The inside of the ear is then clean and free from hair.

This needs to be plucked out, using finger and thumb.

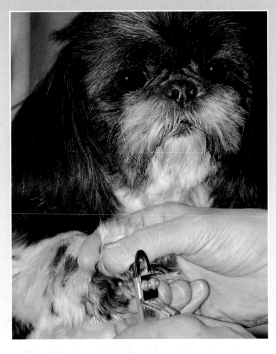

It is important to keep nails trimmed.

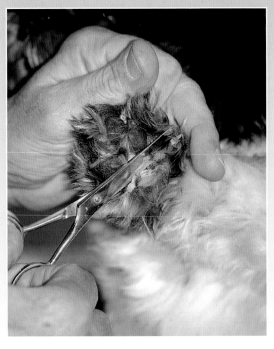

The hair between the pads needs to be trimmed.

ADULT CARE: PET TRIM

If you decide to keep your Shih Tzu in pet trim, your workload will be greatly reduced, but your dog will still need brushing and combing – ideally on a daily basis – to keep his coat in good order. This also gives you the opportunity to give your Shih Tzu a thorough check, which means you will be able to spot any problems at an early stage.

TEETH

You will need to clean your Shih Tzu's teeth on a regular basis, every week. At the same time, examine his gums for redness and teeth for any plaque build-up. Plaque can lead to gum disease, which can be very painful and makes eating difficult, which will affect his general good health. There are many dental chews available nowadays specifically to help with this problem.

EARS

The Shih Tzu's ears are prone to picking up debris, such as grass seeds and leaf litter. These are easy to spot and remove during grooming. It is also important to look inside the ear. Check there is no change in colour or smell. If there is, and particularly if your Shih Tzu is shaking his head or pawing at his ear, consult your vet.

The Shih Tzu grows long strands of hair at the top of the ear canal. These need to be very carefully removed. If you use a professional groomer, these should be removed at each visit, but if you groom your dog at home you will need to learn how to do this regularly by yourself. Initially get someone more experienced to deomonstrate how to do this. Some people use their fingers, others use blunt-ended scissors, but never delve too deeply into the ear as this can cause serious damage.

BATHING

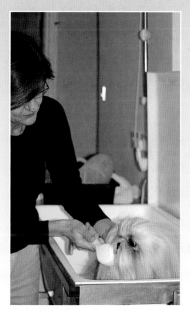

If you start bathing from an early age, your Shih Tzu will become accustomed to the routine.

Wrap your Shih Tzu in a towel and let it absorb the moisture.

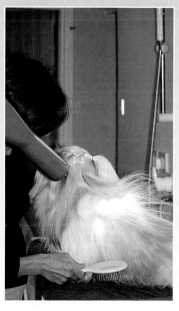

Keep the hair-dryer on a moderate heat, and do not direct it into your dog's face.

NAILS

Get into the habit of checking your Shih Tzu's nails regularly to see if they need trimming. He will have front dewclaws, and possibly back dewclaws as well – these are like our thumbs and will also need trimming. The hair that grows between the pads of his feet also needs attention. This can grow at a considerable rate and become matted, which can make it very painful for a dog to walk.

BATHING

When you bathe your Shih Tzu, use a good-quality dog shampoo and conditioner. Again, there are many products that are available. You could ask the breeder to recommend a particular brand. Do not be tempted to use human products, as they can dry the coat and skin, and always use a 'no tears' shampoo around the eyes and face.

Ensure that you have everything prepared before you start to bathe – there is nothing worse than having a very wet Shih Tzu wrapped in a towel while you run around the house trying to find the equipment you need. Assemble the following:

- Towels

- Three jugs: two mixed with the appropriate amount of shampoo and warm water and the other with conditioner mixed with warm water.
- Brushes
- Combs
- Hairdryer.

Most people have a shower attachment on the bath, which is ideal for bathing a Shih Tzu. You will need a bath mat for him to stand on, or you can soak a hand towel and put that down on the surface of the bath. This will prevent your dog from slipping. Make sure you test the water temperature before you start.

Some people advocate plugging the ears with cotton wool to stop water getting in. However, when I tried this, I got completely soaked by the dog shaking his head trying to remove the cotton wool, so I now take extra care around the inside of the ears. Once you start bathing, follow this procedure:

• Start by ensuring that your Shih Tzu is completely wet. This can sometimes be quite difficult with a very dense coat.
• When he is soaked through, gently pour the shampoo mixture over his body and then massage into the coat.
• Rinse off thoroughly.
• Gently shampoo around the face, using a 'no tears' shampoo. An old face cloth can be used for the face.
• Repeat the process with the second jug of shampoo mixture and rinse again.

• Apply the conditioner, which you have already mixed with warm water, and then rinse off.
• Wrap your Shih Tzu in a towel and gently pat dry. Too much rubbing with the towel will cause matting.

If you are drying a puppy, try to have him on your lap, the same as you would for grooming – preferably with you sitting on the floor as the puppy may try to escape. Using a brush, start with his back and progress to his underside, holding the dryer at a small distance from him. The most awkward part is trying to dry his chest and head, but you just need to be patient and persevere. At first, your puppy may not like the dryer, so keep reassuring him throughout the whole process. A couple of tips: do not direct the dryer into his face, he will not like that at all, and do not have the dryer on full heat. Once your dog is

completely dry, gently comb through his coat, ensuring that you pay attention to the whole of his body and his head.

As your puppy gets older and becomes used to being groomed, bathed and dried, you can progress to grooming on a table with a towel for the dog to lie on, but only when you are confident enough that he will not try to jump off. It does make the process a lot easier, especially on your back.

FULL COAT
A Shih Tzu in full coat looks stunning, but you must be prepared for a lot of hard work to keep the coat at its best. When a Shih Tzu is mature, moulting occurs twice a year with each bitch's season, while males will moult only once, usually around early springtime. It is the woolly undercoat that sheds. You will need to be extra vigilant when grooming at this time, as the coat

PRACTICAL TIPS

If you decide that you want to try keeping your pet Shih Tzu in fairly full coat, there are few tips that could be of help:
• Consider trimming out your dog's armpits and thinning his underside. This will reduce the amount of debris the coat collects.
• Trim the hair around his feet.
• If tying the top-knot is causing problems,

carefully trim the top of the head so your dog ends up with a fringe, but the remaining hair is feathered into his ears and neck.
• To keep his ears and whiskers out of the way when he is eating, try making him a snood out of an old pop sock, or you can buy snoods from many good pet outlets at shows or on the web.

GROOMING: FULL COAT

If you keep your Shih Tzu in full coat, you will need to brush it through, layer by layer, on a daily basis.

After brushing, work through the coat with a wide-toothed comb.

Now repeat the process with narrow-toothed comb.

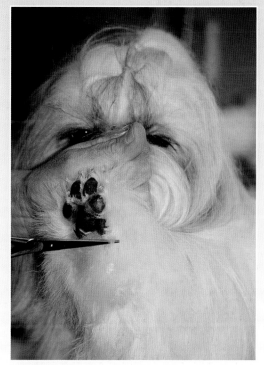

The Shih Tzu is an untrimmed breed, but most groomers will trim around the feet to give a neater appearance.

INFORMAL TOP-KNOT

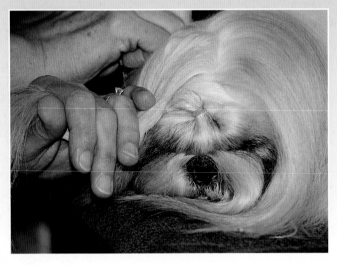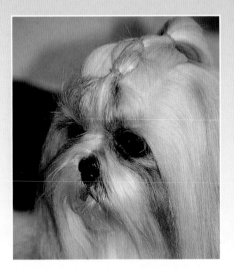

An informal top-knot is used for every day. Most owners have a favourite style.

becomes like cotton-wool and can be very hard to clear of matting. Use a grooming spray to aid the process. Spray it gently through the section you are going to groom, then brush thoroughly. Repeat this process throughout the whole of the coat.

When you return from a walk, check your Shih Tzu's ears, feet and underside for any debris he may have picked up. In the summer, pay particular attention to grass darts. These are nasty things which, because of their structure, do not fall out of the coat. In fact, they work further into the coat, pad or ear and can become imbedded in the skin, leading to an infection and, worse case scenario, an operation to have the grass dart removed.

SHOW PRESENTATION

To stand any chance of success in the show world, your Shih Tzu must be presented to perfection; this is especially true for a long-coated breed. Nowadays exhibitors have access to the very best grooming products and those with top-winning dogs put their all into presentation. Not a day should go by without a show dog's coat being checked over to remove any debris that may cause tangles in between full grooming sessions.

Most exhibitors spend a lot of time learning how to groom their dog correctly for the show ring. Full instructions for grooming to this standard are beyond the scope of this book. If you are interested in doing this, first try

contacting a breed club and speaking to other exhibitors and experienced groomers to see what is involved. Some breed clubs run Shih Tzu grooming seminars, which would be very useful for you to attend.

Most exhibitors bathe their Shih Tzu the day before a show so the coat is in tip-top condition when the dog enters the ring; a clean, gleaming coat enhances every Shih Tzu's other virtues.

Learning to tie the top-knot is important. A correctly placed top-knot can make all the difference to a Shih Tzu's expression; however characteristic your Shih Tzu's head may be, if the top-knot is not tied up correctly, the beauty of it will be ruined.

SHOW PRESENTATION: TYING A SHOW TOP-KNOT

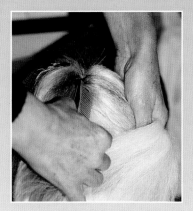

First separate the hair for the top-knot.

Check you have an equal amount of hair from both sides.

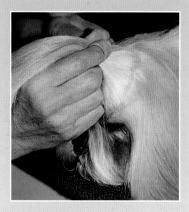

Now tie with a rubber band.

A top-knot ready for the show ring.

Your Shih Tzu's tail should be carried over the back naturally, but in a show situation a little help is sometimes needed from the handler.

The Shih Tzu is an active breed and will enjoy daily outings.

EXERCISE

Taking your Shih Tzu for walks is probably one of the treats of dog ownership that you are looking forward to, but you need to proceed with caution. A puppy will only need very short walks, as too much walking on pavements can affect the bones of a puppy. Their bones are still soft and can become damaged. Playing in the garden is sufficient exercise for a Shih Tzu puppy until he is fully vaccinated. From that point you can gradually inroduce a few minutes of lead-walking every day along with 10 minutes of more energetic exercise. This can be increased over time as your Shih Tzu matures. Young puppies love nothing more than shredding newspaper or playing retrieve with the inside of a toilet roll. Toys can be taken on walks as a form of encouragement with puppies, or for chasing after when they are older and are safe off their lead.

Once your Shih Tzu has reached maturity, he will need a minimum of two 20-minute walks each day, which should include some free-running exercise as well as lead-walking. Try to vary walks and make them more interesting (e.g throwing a ball or playing hide and seek), so that your Shih Tzu gets some mental stimulation as well as physical exercise.

THE IN-SEASON BITCH

If you have a bitch, she will have her first season any time from around six months of age. There are no hard and fast rules as to when this will happen. Some Shih Tzu puppies can be as young as five months, others as old as a year. If you have a very clean bitch, the only sign you may have that she is in season is that she will be constantly licking herself. The normal length of a season is 21 days. During this time, your bitch may go off her food slightly, but do not worry – she will return to normal eating when her season has finished.

You must be very vigilant with your bitch at this time and not let her out into the garden on her own unless it is secure. The smell of a bitch in season can travel for miles, and the last thing you want is for the local male dogs to be beating the fence down. Believe me, some males can be very persistent. Should the unthinkable happen, take your bitch to the vet within 24 hours where she can be given an injection to terminate a possible pregnancy rather than allowing her to produce unplanned puppies; nonetheless, prior to vaccination you must discuss with your vet the possible dangers and side effects of this so-called 'easy way out'.

The average bitch will have two seasons a year, normally about six months apart, but, again, there are no hard and fast rules. Some bitches will go up to a year between seasons, others may have them every five months. Never breed from a bitch that is too young. If you do decide to breed, the third season is the best time to start. If you do not want to breed and are considering having your bitch spayed, talk to your vet. He will explain all the implications and advise you as to when the surgery should be carried out. Normally the advice is to let a bitch have her first season, then spay three months later.

THE MALE SHIH TZU

A male Shih Tzu puppy will start to mature around five months of age. He may become more assertive and dominant. This is when you must let him know that you are the boss. Try regarding him as a teenage boy. He could be full of good ideas but doesn't have a clue how to execute them – therefore, he could, potentially, get himself into all sorts of trouble.

If you start having a problem with his behaviour and you do not plan to show him, consider having him castrated. Your vet will be able to give you more advice.

It is less usual for a male to mark his territory indoors if he hasn't got a bitch he's trying to protect. Outside, he will start to mark where other males have been.

If you have had your Shih Tzu spayed or castrated, the food requirement will be less, so be sure to keep quite a close eye on your dog's weight. The coat may also become thicker, and require more regular grooming.

THE OLDER SHIH TZU
A dog is regarded as being a veteran when he reaches the age of seven years. However, it is quite common for a Shih Tzu to live to 14 or 16 years of age – I recently heard of a Shih Tzu passing away at the grand age of 21. Within the show fraternity there is great respect for our veterans and they are warmly congratulated whenever they 'strut their stuff' around the show ring.

As your Shih Tzu progresses to an older age, you may notice that he requires less exercise. Instead of running around the garden, chasing everything in sight, he may decide he will enjoy a gentle stroll, taking in the different sights and smells. He will still be keen to participate in any outing you may have in mind, but he may need to take it more slowly. Never force him to exercise more than he is physically able.

Keeping the older dog's weight under control is vitally important as old age can have an effect on his joints and heart. There are complete menus that are specifically formulated for older dogs. If you have been feeding one meal a day, it may help his digestive system to convert to two meals. Older dogs can suffer with arthritis the same as we humans; cod liver oil capsules may help, but be cautious, as it may cause an upset stomach. Older Shih Tzu can suffer with many of the complaints that are associated with advancing age. An annual check-up by your vet is still as important. Try to continue to keep his teeth clean, as plaque and gum disease can be very painful and cause problems with eating.

SAYING GOODBYE
If we could choose the way we say goodbye, it would be to come down one morning and find that our beloved Shih Tzu has passed away peacefully in his sleep. Unfortunately, this does not always happen and, sadly, you may have to make the decision to say farewell. This decision is very often reached after consulting with your vet, but whether it is because of illness or old age, it can be the hardest decision you ever have to make. However, it is important that it is your decision. To allow your beautiful Shih Tzu to go with dignity is the kindest and last act of love you can do for him. In a good practice, your vet will be happy to come to your home or you may choose to go to the surgery. Either way, deep in your heart you will know when the time has come.

Some people decide to bury their Shih Tzu in the garden in a favourite place, though if put to sleep at the vet's, many countries' laws do not allow you to take the body home. Others will have a private cremation and scatter the ashes at home. Most vets are now able to offer a burial or cremation service through a pet crematorium. The decision is yours and is a very personal one.

In time, you will have many happy memories of your beautiful Shih Tzu and come to realise that peace is a parting gift.

The older Shih Tzu deserves special consideration.

TRAINING AND SOCIALISATION

Chapter 6

When you decided to bring a Shih Tzu into your home, you probably had dreams of how it would be, sharing your life with such a glamorous breed. A happy, confident and extrovert dog, the Shih Tzu has the makings of being an outstanding companion – but he does not come ready-made. You cannot expect a dog, regardless of whether he is a puppy or an adult, to understand your version of 'right' and 'wrong', and he does not know how to slot into your lifestyle. A Shih Tzu has to learn his place in your family and discover what is acceptable behaviour.

We have a great starting point in that the breed has an outgoing temperament. The Shih Tzu wants to be with people, and he likes to please. He is also highly intelligent, which makes him quick to learn. However, given the chance he will use his intelligence to get his own way – so you will need to make sure you keep one step ahead!

THE FAMILY PACK

Dogs have been domesticated for some 14,000 years, but luckily for us, they have inherited and retained behaviour from their distant ancestor – the wolf. A Shih Tzu may never have lived in the wild, but he is born with the survival skills and the mentality of a meat-eating predator who hunts in a pack. A wolf living in a pack owes its existence to mutual co-operation and an acceptance of a hierarchy, as this ensures both food and protection. A domesticated dog living in a family pack has exactly the same outlook. He wants food, companionship, and leadership – and it is your job to provide for these needs.

YOUR ROLE

Theories about dog behaviour and methods of training go in and out of fashion, but in reality, nothing has changed from the day when wolves ventured in from the wild to join the family circle. The wolf (and equally the dog) accepts a subservient place in the family pack in return for food and protection. In a dog's eyes, you are his leader and he relies on you to make all the important decisions. This does not mean that you have to act like a dictator or a bully. You are accepted as a leader, without argument, as long as you have the right credentials.

The first part of the job is easy. You are the provider and you are therefore respected because you supply food. In a Shih Tzu's eyes, you must be the ultimate hunter, because a day never goes by when you cannot find food. The second part of the leader's job description is straightforward, but for some reason we find it hard to achieve. In order for a dog to accept his place in the family pack, he must respect his leader as the decision-maker. A low-ranking pack animal does not question authority; he is perfectly happy to see someone else shoulder the responsibility. Problems will only arise if you cut a poor figure as leader and the dog feels he should mount a challenge for the top-ranking role.

HOW TO BE A GOOD LEADER

There are a number of guidelines to follow to establish yourself in the role of leader in a way that your Shih Tzu understands and respects. If you have a puppy, you may think you don't have to take this on board for a few months, but that would be a big mistake. With a Shih Tzu it is absolutely essential to start as you mean to go on. The behaviour he learns as a puppy will continue throughout his adult life, which means that undesirable behaviour can be very difficult to rectify.

Have you got what it takes to be a firm, fair and consistent leader?

When your Shih Tzu first arrives in his new home, follow these guidelines:
- **Keep it simple:** Decide on the rules you want your Shih Tzu to obey and always make it 100 per cent clear what is acceptable, and what is unacceptable, behaviour.
- **Be consistent:** If you are not consistent about enforcing rules, how can you expect your

Shih Tzu to take you seriously? There is nothing worse than allowing your Shih Tzu to jump on the sofa one moment and then scolding him the next time he does it because he is muddy. As far as the Shih Tzu is concerned, he may as well try it on because he can't predict your reaction. Bear in mind, inconsistency leads to insecurity.
- **Get your timing right:** If you are rewarding your Shih Tzu and equally if you are reprimanding him, you must respond within one to two seconds otherwise the dog will not link his behaviour with your reaction (see page 93).
- **Read your dog's body language:** Find out how to read body language and facial expressions (see page 91) so that you understand your Shih Tzu's feelings and intentions.
- **Be aware of your own body language:** You can help your dog to learn by using your body language to communicate with him. For example, if you want your dog to come to you, open your arms out and look inviting. If you want your dog to stay, use a hand signal (palm flat, facing the dog) so you are effectively 'blocking' his advance.

- **Tone of voice:** Dogs do not speak English; they learn by associating a word with the required action. However, they are very receptive to tone of voice, so you can use your voice to praise him or to correct undesirable behaviour. If you are pleased with your Shih Tzu, praise him to the skies in a warm, happy voice. If you want to stop him raiding the bin, use a deep, stern voice when you say "No".

- **Give one command only** for each thing you want to convey. If you keep repeating a command, or keep changing it, your Shih Tzu will think you are babbling and will probably ignore you. If your Shih Tzu does not respond the first time you ask, make it simple by using a treat to lure him into position and then you can reward him for a correct response.

- **Daily reminders:** A young, cheeky Shih Tzu is apt to forget his manners from time to time and an adolescent dog may attempt to challenge your authority (see page 102). Rather than coming down on your Shih Tzu like a ton of bricks when he does something wrong, try to prevent bad manners by daily reminders of good manners. For example:

i. Do not let your dog barge ahead of you when you are going through a door.

ii Do not let him leap out of the car the moment you open the door (which could be potentially lethal, as well as being disrespectful).

iii. Do not let him eat from your hand when you are at the table.

iv. Do not let him 'win' a toy at the end of a play session and then make off with it. You 'own' his toys and you 'allow' him to play with them. Your Shih Tzu must learn to give up a toy when you ask.

UNDERSTANDING YOUR SHIH TZU

Body language is an important means of communication between dogs, which they use to make friends, to assert status and to avoid conflict. It is important to get on your dog's wavelength by understanding his body language and reading his facial expressions. This can be difficult in a long-coated dog, but if you are observant, you will start to learn the way your dog responds to different situations.

- A positive body posture and a wagging tail indicate a happy, confident dog.

- A crouched body posture with ears back and tail down show that a dog is being submissive. A dog may do this when he is being told off or if a more assertive dog approaches him.

- A bold dog will stand tall, looking strong and alert. His ears will be forward and his tail will be held high.

- A playful dog will go down on his front legs while standing on his hind legs in a bow position. This friendly invitation says: "I'm no threat, let's play."

If you spend time observing your Shih Tzu, you will be able to interpret his moods and feelings.

- An assertive, aggressive dog will meet other dogs with a hard stare. If he is challenged, he may bare his teeth and growl, and the corners of his mouth will be drawn forward. His ears will be forward and he will appear tense in every muscle.
- A nervous dog will often show aggressive behaviour as a means of self-protection. If threatened, this dog will lower his head and flatten his ears. The corners of his mouth may be drawn back and he may bark or whine.
- Some Shih Tzu are 'smilers', curling up their top lip and showing their teeth when they greet people. This should never be confused with a snarl, which would be accompanied by the upright posture of a dominant dog. A smiling dog will have a low body posture and a wagging tail; he is being submissive and it is a greeting that is often used when low-ranking animals greet high-ranking animals in a pack.
- Watch out for the Shih Tzu speciality –your dog will take off for no reason and sprint round the room or the garden like a wild thing before coming

You need to find out what is the best reward for your Shih Tzu.

to rest. Whether this is an exhibition of high spirits or the Shih Tzu's way of letting off steam is a matter for conjecture.

GIVING REWARDS

Why should your Shih Tzu do as you ask? If you follow the guidelines given above, your Shih Tzu should respect your authority, but what about the time when he is playing with a new doggy friend or has found a really enticing scent? The answer is that you must always be the

most interesting, the most attractive and the most irresistible person in your Shih Tzu's eyes. It would be nice to think that you could achieve this by personality alone, but most of us need a little extra help. You need to find out what is the biggest reward for your dog. Shih Tzu love their food, and most will be keen to work for a tasty treat. However, there are Shih Tzu who become focused on a favourite toy – and a game with this 'treasure' may be seen as the best reward. But whatever reward you use, make sure it is something that your dog really wants.

When you are teaching a dog a new exercise, you should reward your Shih Tzu frequently. When he knows the exercise or command, reward him randomly so that he keeps on responding to you in a positive manner.

If your Shih Tzu does something extra special, like leaving an interesting scent and coming the moment you call, make sure he knows how pleased you are by giving him a handful of treats or having an extra-long play with his favourite toy. If he gets a bonanza reward, he is more likely to come back on future occasions because you have proved to be even more rewarding than his previous activity.

TOP TREATS

Some trainers grade treats depending on what they are asking the dog to do. A dog may get a low-grade treat (such as a piece of dry food) to reward good behaviour on a random basis, such as sitting when you open a door or allowing you to examine his teeth. High-grade treats (which may be cooked liver, sausage or cheese) may be reserved for training new exercises, or for use in the park when you want a really good recall, for example.

Whatever type of treat you use, you should remember to subtract it from your Shih Tzu's daily food ration. Shih Tzu can be prone to obesity. Fat dogs are lethargic, prone to health problems and will almost certainly have a shorter life expectancy, so reward your Shih Tzu, but always keep a check on his figure!

HOW DO DOGS LEARN?

It is not difficult to get inside your Shih Tzu's head and understand how he learns, as it is not dissimilar to the way we learn. Dogs learn by conditioning: they find out that specific behaviours produce specific consequences. This is known as operant conditioning or consequence learning. Consequences have to be immediate or clearly linked to the behaviour, as a dog sees the world in terms of action and result. Dogs will quickly learn if an action has a bad consequence or a good consequence.

Dogs also learn by association. This is known as classical conditioning or association learning. It is the type of learning made famous by Pavlov's experiment with dogs. Pavlov presented dogs with food and measured their salivary response (how much they drooled). Then he rang a bell just before presenting the food. At first, the dogs did not salivate until the food was presented. But after a while they learnt that the sound of the bell meant that food was coming and so they salivated when they heard the bell. A dog needs to learn the association in order for it to have any meaning. For example, a dog that has never seen a lead before will be completely indifferent to it. A dog that has learnt that a lead means he is going for a walk will get excited the second he sees the lead; he has learnt to associate a lead with a walk.

BE POSITIVE

The most effective method of training dogs is to use their ability to learn by consequence and to teach that the behaviour you want produces a good consequence. For example, if you ask your Shih Tzu to "Sit" and reward him with a treat, he will learn that it is worth his while to sit on command because it will lead to a treat. He is far more likely to repeat the behaviour, and the behaviour will become stronger, because it results in a positive outcome. This method of training is known as positive reinforcement and it generally leads to a happy, co-operative dog that is willing to work and a handler who has fun training their dog.

Some Shih Tzu prefer to be rewarded with a game rather than a food treat.

THE CLICKER REVOLUTION

Karen Pryor pioneered the technique of clicker training when she was working with dolphins. It is very much a continuation of Pavlov's work and makes full use of association learning. Karen wanted to mark 'correct' behaviour at the precise moment it happened. She found it was impossible to toss a fish to a dolphin when it was in mid-air, when she wanted to reward it. Her aim was to establish a conditioned response so the dolphin knew that it had performed correctly and a reward would follow.

The solution was the clicker: a small matchbox-shaped training aid, with a metal tongue that makes a click when it is pressed. To begin with, the dolphin had to learn that a click meant that food was coming. The dolphin then learnt that it must 'earn' a click in order to get a reward. Clicker training has been used with many different animals, most particularly with dogs, and it has proved hugely successful. It is a great aid for pet owners and is also widely used by professional trainers who are training highly specialised skills.

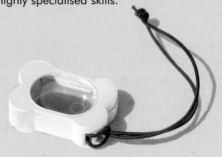

The opposite approach is negative reinforcement. This is far less effective and often results in a poor relationship between dog and owner. In this method of training, you ask your Shih Tzu to "Sit" and if he does not respond, you deliver a sharp yank on the training collar or push his rear to the ground. The dog learns that not responding to your command has a bad consequence and he may be less likely to ignore you in the future. However, it may well have a bad consequence for you, too. A dog that is treated in this way may associate harsh handling with the handler and become aggressive or fearful. Instead of establishing a pattern of willing co-operation, you are establishing a relationship built on coercion.

GETTING STARTED

As you train your Shih Tzu, you will develop your own techniques as you get to know what motivates him. You may decide to get involved with clicker training or you may prefer to go for a simple command-and-reward formula. It does not matter what form of training you use, as long as it is based on positive, reward-based methods.

There are a few important guidelines to bear in mind when you are training your Shih Tzu:

- Find a training area that is free from distractions, particularly when you are just starting out. Shih Tzu can become easily distracted by noise and by scent, so it may be easier to train him indoors to begin with.
- Keep training sessions short, especially with young puppies that have very short attention spans.
- Do not train if you are in a bad mood or if you are on a tight schedule – the training session will be doomed to failure.
- If you are using a toy as a reward, make sure it is only

available when you are training. In this way it has an added value for your Shih Tzu.

- If you are using food treats, make sure they are bite-size and easy to swallow; you don't want to hang about while your Shih Tzu chews on his treat.
- Do not attempt to train your Shih Tzu after he has eaten, after a lengthy grooming session, or soon after returning from exercise. He will either be too full up to care about food treats or too tired to concentrate.
- When you are training, move around your allocated area so that your dog does not think that an exercise can only be performed in one place.
- The Shih Tzu has a stubborn streak and if he finds an exercise difficult, he may dig his heels in and refuse to co-operate. Do not get stressed, and, most especially, do not get confrontational. Go back to basics, or break the exercise down into simple stages so your Shih Tzu can be rewarded for making some progress. Have a break – and you will probably find your Shih Tzu is more successful when you try again at the next training session.
- If a training session is not going well – either because you are in the wrong frame of mind or the dog is not focusing – ask your Shih Tzu to do something you know he can do (such as a trick he enjoys performing) and then you can reward him with a food treat or a play with his favourite toy, ending the session on a happy, positive note.
- Do not train for too long. You need to end a training session on a high, with your Shih Tzu wanting more, rather than making him sour by asking too much from him.

In the exercises that follow, clicker training is introduced and followed, but all the exercises will work without the use of a clicker.

INTRODUCING A CLICKER

This is dead easy, and the intelligent Shih Tzu will learn about the clicker in record time! It can be combined with attention training, which is a very useful tool and can be used on many different occasions.

- Prepare some treats and go to an area that is free from distractions. Allow your Shih Tzu to wander and when he stops to look at you, click and reward by throwing him a treat. This means he will not crowd you, but will go looking for the treat. Repeat a couple of times. If your Shih Tzu is very easily distracted, you may need to start this exercise with the dog on a lead.
- After a few clicks, your Shih Tzu will understand that if he hears a click, he will get a treat. He must now learn that he must 'earn' a click. This time, when your Shih Tzu looks at you, wait a little longer before clicking and then reward him. If your Shih Tzu is on a lead but responding well, try him off the lead.
- When your Shih Tzu is working for a click and giving you his attention, you can introduce a cue or command word, such as "Watch". Repeat a few times, using the cue. You now have a Shih Tzu that understands the clicker and will give you his attention when you ask him to "Watch".

It does not take the clever Shih Tzu long to learn that a click means a reward will follow.

The Sit is the easiest exercise to teach, and is useful in many different situations.

To start with lure your Shih Tzu into the Down. He will then learn to respond to the verbal cue.

TRAINING EXERCISES

THE SIT

This is the easiest exercise to teach, so it is rewarding for both you and your Shih Tzu.

- Choose a tasty treat and hold it just above your puppy's nose. As he looks up at the treat, he will naturally 'Sit'. As soon as he is in position, reward him.
- Repeat the exercise and when your pup understands what you want, introduce the "Sit" command.
- You can practise the Sit exercise at mealtimes by holding out the bowl and waiting for your dog to sit. Most Shih Tzu learn this one very quickly!

THE DOWN

Work hard at this exercise because a reliable 'Down' is useful in many different situations, and an instant 'Down' can be a lifesaver. When you are grooming your Shih Tzu, life will be so much easier if you have a dog that will lie down on request.

- You can start with your dog in a 'Sit', or it is just as effective to teach it when the dog is standing. Hold a treat just below your puppy's nose and slowly lower it towards the ground. The treat acts as a lure and your puppy will follow it, first going down on his forequarters and then bringing his hindquarters down as he tries to get the treat.
- Make sure you close your fist around the treat and only reward your puppy with the treat when he is in the correct position. If your puppy is reluctant to go 'Down', you can apply gentle pressure on his shoulders to encourage him to go into the correct position.
- When your puppy is following the treat and going into position, introduce a verbal command.
- Build up this exercise over a period of time, each time waiting a little longer before giving the reward, so the puppy learns to stay in the 'Down' position.

THE RECALL

The Shih Tzu is not a believer in instant obedience, and recalls might not always be lightning fast. However, the aim is to have a dog that is happy to respond because he knows there's a good chance of getting a reward.

- Hopefully, the breeder will have already started recall training by calling the puppies in from outside and rewarding them with some treats scattered on the floor. But even if this has not been the case, you will find that a puppy arriving in his new home is naturally tuned into responding to the human voice. His chief desire is to follow you and to be with you. Capitalise on this from day one by getting your pup's attention and calling him to you in a bright, excited tone of voice.
- Practise in the garden. When your puppy is busy exploring, get his attention by calling his name, and, as he runs towards you, introduce the verbal command "Come". Make sure you sound happy and exciting, so your puppy wants to come to you. When he responds, give him lots of praise.
- If your puppy is slow to respond, try running away a few paces or jumping up and down. It doesn't matter how silly you look, the key issue is to get your puppy's attention and then make yourself irresistible!
- In a dog's mind, coming when called should be regarded as the best fun because he knows he is always going to be rewarded. Never make the mistake of telling your dog off, no matter how slow he is to respond, as you will undo all your previous hard work.
- When you call your Shih Tzu to you, make sure he comes up close enough to be touched. He must understand that "Come" means that he should come right up to you, otherwise he will think that he can approach and then veer off when it suits him.
- When you are free-running your dog, make sure you have his favourite toy or a pocket full of treats so you can reward him at intervals throughout the walk when you call him to you. Do not allow your dog to free run and only call him back at the end of the walk to clip on his lead.

SECRET WEAPON

You can build up a strong recall by using another form of association learning. Buy a whistle and when you are giving your Shih Tzu his food, peep on the whistle. You can choose the type of signal you want to give: two short peeps or one long whistle, for example. Within a matter of days, your dog will learn that the sound of the whistle means that food is coming.

Now transfer the lesson outside. Arm yourself with some tasty treats and the whistle. Allow your Shih Tzu to run free in the garden, and, after a couple of minutes, use the whistle. The dog has already learnt to associate the whistle with food, so he will come towards you.

Immediately reward him with a treat and lots of praise. Repeat the lesson a few times in the garden, so you are confident that your dog is responding before trying it in the park. Make sure you always have some treats in your pocket when you go for a walk and your dog will quickly learn how rewarding it is to come to you.

An intelligent Shih Tzu will soon realise that the recall means the end of his walk and then the end of his fun – so who can blame him for not wanting to come back?

TRAINING LINE

This is the equivalent of a very long lead, which you can buy at a pet store, or you can make your own with a length of rope. The training line is attached to your Shih Tzu's collar and should be around 15 feet (4.5 metres) in length.

The purpose of the training line is to prevent your Shih Tzu from disobeying you so that he never has the chance to get into bad habits. For example, when you call your Shih Tzu and he ignores you, you can immediately pick up the end of the training line and call him again. By picking up the line you will have attracted his attention and if you call in an excited, happy voice, your Shih Tzu will come to you. The moment he reaches you, give him a tasty treat so he is instantly rewarded for making the 'right' decision.

The training line is very useful when your Shih Tzu becomes an adolescent and is testing your leadership. When you have reinforced the correct behaviour a number of times, your dog will build up a reliable recall and you will not need to use a training line.

WALKING ON A LOOSE LEAD

This is a simple exercise, as long as you start training from an early

Make yourself sound exciting so your Shih Tzu wants to come to you.

age. A Shih Tzu is very adaptable and will quickly get used to a collar and lead – but if you wait until your pup has finished his vaccination course before you start work, you may find yourself in trouble. A Shih Tzu may resent the feeling of restraint, which he has not been used to, and may respond by doing his own imitation of a bolting horse. You now have twice the workload, as you have to give your pup reassurance as well as teaching him to walk on a loose lead.

In this exercise, as with all lessons that you teach your Shih Tzu, you must adopt a calm, determined, no-nonsense attitude

so he knows that you mean business. This is a 'thinking' dog, and if he does not see why he is being asked to behave in a certain way, he may start thinking for himself and make up his own agenda. You need to earn your dog's respect and make sure you reward him frequently so that he is happy to co-operate with you.

- In the early stages of lead training, allow your puppy to pick his route and follow him. He will get used to the feeling of being 'attached' to you and has no reason to put up any resistance.

- Next, find a toy or a tasty treat and show it to your puppy. Let him follow the treat/toy for a few paces and then reward him.

- Build up the amount of time your pup will walk with you and when he is walking nicely by your side, introduce the verbal command "Heel" or "Close". Give lots of praise when your pup is in the correct position.

- When your pup is walking alongside you, keep focusing his attention on you by using his name and then rewarding him when he looks at you. If it is going well, introduce some changes of direction.

- Do not attempt to take your puppy out on the lead until you have mastered the basics at home. You need to be confident that your puppy accepts the lead and will focus his attention on you, when requested, before you face the challenge of a busy environment.

To begin with you can practise lead training in the garden.

You can teach your Shih Tzu to "Stay" in a Sit, a Stand or a Down.

- If you are heading somewhere special, such as the park, your Shih Tzu will probably try to pull because he is impatient to get there. If this happens, stop, call your dog to you, and do not set off again until he is in the correct position. It may take time, but your Shih Tzu will eventually realise that it is more productive to walk by your side than to pull ahead.

STAYS

This may not be the most exciting exercise, but it is one of the most useful. On this point, a Shih Tzu will disagree because he would always prefer to stay close by you rather than being left – even if it is only for a limited length of time. However, it is important to teach this exercise, as there are many occasions when using a Stay command is a matter of safety. The classic example is when you want your Shih Tzu to stay in the back of the car until you have clipped on his lead.

Some trainers use the verbal command "Stay" when the dog is to stay in position for an extended period of time and "Wait" if the dog is to stay in position for a few seconds until you give the next command. Others trainers use a universal "Stay" to cover all situations. It all comes down to personal preference, and as long as you are consistent, your dog will understand the command he is given.

- Put your puppy in a 'Sit' or a 'Down' and use a hand signal (flat palm, facing the dog) to show he is to stay in position. Step a pace away from the dog. Wait a second, step back and reward him. If you have a lively pup, you may find it easier to train this exercise on the lead.
- Repeat the exercise, gradually increasing the distance you can leave your dog. When you return to your dog's side, praise him quietly and release him with a command, such as "OK".
- Remember to keep your body language very still when you are training this exercise and avoid eye contact with your dog. Work on this exercise over a period of time and you will build up a really reliable Stay.

SOCIALISATION

While your Shih Tzu is mastering basic obedience exercises, there is other, equally important work to do with him. A Shih Tzu is not only becoming a part of your home and family, he is becoming a member of the community. He needs to be able to live in the outside world, coping calmly with every new situation that comes his way. It is your job to introduce him to as many different experiences as possible and to encourage him to behave in an appropriate manner.

In order to socialise your Shih Tzu effectively, it is helpful to understand how his brain is developing and then you will get a perspective on how he sees the world.

CANINE SOCIALISATION
(Birth to 7 weeks)
This is the time when a dog learns how to be a dog. By interacting with his mother and his littermates, a young pup learns about leadership and submission. He learns to read body posture so that he understands the intentions of his mother and his siblings. A puppy that is taken away from his litter too early may always have behavioural problems with other dogs, either being fearful or aggressive.

SOCIALISATION PERIOD
(7 to 12 weeks)
This is the time to get cracking

At around four months, your Shih Tzu will show increasing signs of independence.

and introduce your Shih Tzu puppy to as many different experiences as possible. This includes meeting different people, other dogs and animals, seeing new sights and hearing a range of sounds, from the vacuum cleaner to the roar of traffic. A puppy learns very quickly and what he learns will stay with him for the rest of his life. This is the best time for a puppy to move to a new home, as he is adaptable and ready to form deep bonds.

FEAR-IMPRINT PERIOD
(8 to 11 weeks)
This occurs during the socialisation period and it can be the cause of problems if it is not

handled carefully. If a pup is exposed to a frightening or painful experience, it will lead to lasting impressions. Obviously, you will attempt to avoid frightening situations, such as your pup being bullied by a mean-spirited older dog, or a firework going off, but you cannot always protect your puppy from the unexpected. If your pup has a nasty experience, the best plan is to make light of it and distract him by offering him a treat or a game. The pup will take the lead from you and will be reassured that there is nothing to worry about. If you mollycoddle him and sympathise with him, he is far more likely to retain the memory of his fear.

SENIORITY PERIOD
(12 to 16 weeks)
During this period, your Shih Tzu puppy starts to cut the apron strings and becomes more independent. He will test out his status to find out who is the pack leader: him or you. Bad habits, such as play biting, which may have been seen as endearing a few weeks earlier, should be firmly discouraged. Remember to use positive, reward-based training, but make sure your puppy knows that you are the leader and must be respected.

SECOND FEAR-IMPRINT
PERIOD (6 to 14 months)
This period is not as critical as the first fear-imprint period, but it

should still be handled carefully. During this time your Shih Tzu may appear apprehensive, or he may show fear of something familiar. You may feel as if you have taken a backwards step, but if you adopt a calm, positive manner, your Shih Tzu will see that there is nothing to be frightened of. Do not make your dog confront the thing that frightens him. Simply distract his attention and give him something else to think about, such as obeying a simple command, such as "Sit" or "Down". This will give you the opportunity to praise and reward your dog and will help to boost his confidence.

YOUNG ADULTHOOD AND MATURITY (1 to 4 years)
The timing of this phase depends on the size of the dog: the bigger the dog, the later it is. This period coincides with a dog's increased size and strength, mental as well as physical. Some dogs, particularly those with an assertive nature, will test your leadership again and may become aggressive towards other dogs. Firmness and continued training are essential at this time, so that your Shih Tzu accepts his status in the family pack.

IDEAS FOR SOCIALISATION
When you are socialising your Shih Tzu, you want him to experience as many different situations as possible. Try out

A well socialised Shih Tzu will be calm and confident in all situations.

some of the following ideas, which will ensure your Shih Tzu has an all-round education.

If you are taking on a rescued dog and have little knowledge of his background, it is important to work through a programme of socialisation. A young puppy soaks up new experiences like a sponge, but an older dog can still learn. If a rescued dog shows fear or apprehension, treat him in exactly the same way as you would treat a youngster who is going through the second fear-imprint period.

- Accustom your puppy to household noises, such as the vacuum cleaner, the television and the washing machine.
- Ask visitors to come to the door, wearing different types of clothing – for example, wearing

a hat, a long raincoat, or carrying a stick or an umbrella.

- If you do not have children at home, make sure your Shih Tzu has a chance to meet and play with them. Go to a local park and watch children in the play area. You will not be able to take your Shih Tzu inside the play area, but he will see children playing and will get used to their shouts of excitement.
- Attend puppy classes. These are designed for puppies between the ages of 12 to 20 weeks and give puppies a chance to play and interact together in a controlled, supervised environment. Your vet will have details of a local class.
- Take a walk around some quiet streets, such as a residential area, so your Shih Tzu can get used to the sound of traffic. As he becomes more confident, progress to busier areas. Remember, your lead is like a live wire and your feelings will travel directly to your Shih Tzu. Assume a calm, confident manner and your puppy will take the lead from you and have no reason to be fearful.
- Go to a railway station. You don't have to get on a train if you don't need to, but your Shih Tzu will have the chance to experience trains, people wheeling luggage, loudspeaker announcements, and going up and down stairs and over railway bridges.

- If you live in the town, plan a trip to the country. You can enjoy a day out and provide an opportunity for your Shih Tzu to see livestock, such as sheep, cattle and horses.
- One of the best places for socialising a dog is at a country fair. There will be crowds of people, livestock in pens, tractors, bouncy castles, fairground rides and food stalls.
- When your dog is over 20 weeks of age, locate a training class for adult dogs. You may find that your local training class has both puppy and adult classes.

As your Shih Tzu starts to mature, he may question his place in the family hierarchy.

THE ADOLESCENT SHIH TZU

It happens to every dog – and every owner. One minute you have an obedient well-behaved youngster and the next you have an adolescent who appears to have forgotten everything he ever learnt.

A Shih Tzu male will show adolescent behaviour at around 10 months of age. In terms of behavioural changes, a male may become more assertive as he pushes the boundaries to see if he can challenge your authority. This may also be the case if he is living with other dogs and he fancies increasing his ranking in the pecking order.

The time at which a bitch has her first season is very variable, and could be at any stage between 6 and 12 months. At this stage, a bitch will experience hormonal changes, but she rarely shows a major change in personality. However, she may have the urge to elevate her status at this time and she may well take to pleasing herself rather than trying to co-operate with you.

This can be a trying time, but it is important to retain a sense of perspective. Look at the situation from the dog's perspective and respond to uncharacteristic behaviour with firmness and consistency. Just like a teenager, an adolescent Shih Tzu may feel the need to flex his muscles and challenge the status quo. But if you show that you are a strong leader (see page 90) and are quick to reward good behaviour, your Shih Tzu will be happy to accept you as his protector and provider.

It is important to note that the Shih Tzu is a slow maturing breed, and you would not expect a male or a female to be fully mature in terms of both body and coat, until four years of age.

WHEN THINGS GO WRONG

Positive, reward-based training has proved to be the most effective method of teaching dogs, but what happens when your Shih Tzu does something

TRAINING CLUBS

There are lots of training clubs to choose from. Your vet will probably have details of clubs in your area, or you can ask friends who have dogs if they attend a club. Alternatively, use the internet to find out more information. But how do you know if the club is any good?

Before you take your dog, ask if you can go to a class as an observer and find out the following:
• What experience does the instructor(s) have?
• Do they have experience with Shih Tzu?
• Is the class well organised and are the dogs reasonably quiet? (A noisy class indicates an unruly atmosphere, which will not be conducive to learning.)
• Are there are a number of classes to suit dogs of different ages and abilities?
• Are positive, reward-based training methods used?
• Does the club train for the Good Citizen Scheme (see page 109)?

If you are not happy with the training club, find another one. An inexperienced instructor who cannot handle a number of dogs in a confined environment can do more harm than good.

wrong and you need to show him that his behaviour is unacceptable? The old-fashioned school of dog training used to rely on the powers of punishment and negative reinforcement. A dog who raided the bin, for example, was smacked. Now we have learnt that it is not only unpleasant and cruel to hit a dog, it is also ineffective. If you hit a dog for stealing, he is more than likely to see you as the bad consequence of stealing, so he may raid the bin again, but probably not when you are around. If he raided the bin some time before you discovered it, he will be even more confused by your punishment, as he will not relate your response to his 'crime'.

A more commonplace example is when a dog fails to respond to a recall in the park. When the dog eventually comes back, the owner puts the dog on the lead and goes straight home to punish the dog for his poor response. Unfortunately, the dog will have a different interpretation. He does not think: "I won't ignore a recall command because the bad consequence is the end of my play in the park." He thinks: "Coming to my owner resulted in the end of playtime – therefore coming to my owner has a bad consequence, so I won't do that again."

There are a number of strategies to tackle undesirable behaviour – and they have nothing to do with harsh handling.

Ignoring bad behaviour: The Shih Tzu has a big personality – and his chief desire is to be with people. So, if you cannot give attention – because you are busy in the kitchen, for example – your Shih Tzu may demand it and will bark until he gets his own way. The intelligent Shih Tzu believes he can change a situation simply by making a noise – and even if you tell him off, he will still see this as a form of attention.

In this situation, the best and most effective response is to ignore your Shih Tzu. Turn your back, do not speak to him, and, most important of all, avoid eye contact. Wait until your Shih Tzu is calm and quiet, and then give a little low-key attention – maybe asking for a Sit or a Down, so you

A Shih Tzu must learn that he cannot demand attention by jumping up or by barking.

As soon as the dog ceases to demand attention, he can be rewarded.

can reward his 'good' behaviour. Repeat this on every occasion when your Shih Tzu barks for attention, and he will soon learn that barking is non-productive. He is not rewarded with your attention; in fact, being quiet is the most effective strategy because this is when he gets your attention. In this scenario, you have not only taught your Shih Tzu that barking will not work for him, you have also earned his respect because you have taken control of the situation.

Stopping bad behaviour: There are occasions when you want to call an instant halt to whatever it is your Shih Tzu is doing. He may have just jumped on the sofa, or you may have caught him red-handed in the rubbish bin. He has already committed the 'crime', so your aim is to stop him and to redirect his attention. You can do this by using a deep, firm tone of voice to say "No", which will startle him, and then call him to you in a bright, happy voice. If necessary, you can attract him with a toy or a treat. The moment your Shih Tzu stops the undesirable behaviour and comes towards you, you can reward his good behaviour. You can back this up by running through a couple of simple

exercises, and rewarding him with treats or a game with his toy. In this way, your Shih Tzu focuses his attention on you and sees you as the greatest source of reward and pleasure.

In a more extreme situation, when you want to interrupt undesirable behaviour and you know that a simple "No" will not do the trick, you can try something a little more dramatic. If you get a can and fill it with pebbles, it will make a really loud noise when you shake it or throw it. The same effect can be achieved with purpose-made training discs. The dog will be startled and stop what he is doing. Even better, the dog will not associate the unpleasant noise with you. This gives you the perfect opportunity to be the nice guy, calling the dog to you and giving him lots of praise.

PROBLEM BEHAVIOUR

If you have trained your Shih Tzu from puppyhood, survived his adolescence and established yourself as a fair and consistent leader, you will end up with a brilliant companion dog. The Shih Tzu is a confident, well-balanced dog, who rarely has hang-ups if he has been correctly reared and socialised. The most common reason for problem behaviour among Shih Tzu is over-indulgent, inconsistent owners. An owner who spoils and pampers a Shih Tzu will end up with a dog who seeks to take advantage – and the Shih Tzu can be very clever and manipulative when he wants to get his own way. This does not make a dog happy. In the vast majority of cases, a Shih Tzu would prefer to hand over the decisions to you so he can live peaceably in his family pack. However, if you fail to establish the correct hierarchy, your Shih Tzu will feel he must take on the role of leader.

If you have taken on a rescued Shih Tzu, it may be that you are having to cope with established behavioural problems that are the result of poor management in a

If you have taken on an older dog, you may need to reshape his behaviour.

former home. If this is the case, or if you are worried about your Shih Tzu and feel out of your depth, do not delay in seeking professional help. This is readily available, usually through a referral from your vet, or you can find out additional information on the internet (see Appendices for web addresses). An animal behaviourist will have experience in tackling problem behaviour and will be able to help both you and your dog.

RESOURCE GUARDING

If you have trained and socialised your Shih Tzu correctly, he will know his place in the family pack and will have no desire to challenge your authority. If you have taken on a rescued dog who has not been trained and

socialised, or if you have been inconsistent in handling your Shih Tzu, you may find you have problems with an assertive dog.

It is a mistake to believe that it is only the big, macho breeds, such as Rottweilers or German Shepherd Dogs, that show overly assertive behaviour. Certainly, a big dog has the muscle to back up his feelings, but, in fact, dominance is expressed in many different ways, which may include the following:
• Showing lack of respect for your personal space. For example, your Shih Tzu will always be prancing at your heels, or running ahead so he can go through doors ahead of you.
• Ignoring basic obedience commands.
• Showing no respect to younger members of the family, jumping up at them, mouthing them or trying to steal their toys.
• A male dog may start marking (cocking his leg) in the house.
• Aggression towards people or other dogs (see page 108).

However, the most common behaviour displayed by a Shih Tzu who has ideas above his station is resource guarding. This may take a number of different forms:
• Getting up on to the sofa or your favourite armchair and growling when you tell him to get back on the floor.
• Becoming possessive over a toy,

Sometimes a Shih Tzu will become possessive over his toys and refuse to give them up.

Your Shih Tzu needs to learn that you 'own' his toys, and he is not allowed to guard them.

or guarding his food bowl by growling when you get too close.

- Growling when anyone approaches his bed or when anyone gets too close to where he is lying.

In each of these scenarios, the Shih Tzu has something he values and he aims to keep it. He does not have sufficient respect for you, his human leader, to give up what he wants and he is 'warning' you to keep away.

If you see signs of your Shih Tzu behaving in this way, you must work at lowering his status so that he realises that you are the leader and he must accept your authority. Although you need to be firm, you also need to use positive training methods so that your Shih Tzu is rewarded for the behaviour you want. In

this way, his 'correct' behaviour will be strengthened and repeated.

The golden rule is not to become confrontational. The dog will see this as a challenge and may become even more determined not to co-operate. There are a number of steps you can take to lower your Shih Tzu's status, which are far more likely to have a successful outcome. They include:

- Go back to basics and hold daily training sessions. Make sure you have some really tasty treats, or find a toy your Shih Tzu really values and only bring it out at training sessions. Run through all the training exercises you have taught your Shih Tzu, making it a fun session, which will give him mental stimulation and allow you the opportunity to make a

big fuss of him and reward him when he does well. This will help to reinforce the message that you are the leader and that it is rewarding to do as you ask.

- Teach your Shih Tzu something new; this can be as simple as learning a trick, such as begging or shaking paws. A Shih Tzu loves to show off, and he will benefit from interacting with you.
- Be 100 per cent consistent with all house rules – your Shih Tzu must never sit on the sofa (unless that is something you don't mind him doing) and you must never allow him to guard his favourite toy. The quick-thinking Shih Tzu will sum up a situation in a split second, and if he senses weakness or inconsistency, he will be swift to take advantage.
- If your Shih Tzu is becoming

possessive over toys, remove all his toys and keep them out of reach. It is then up to you to decide when to produce a toy and to initiate a game. Equally, it is you who will decide when the game is over and when to remove the toy. This teaches your Shih Tzu that you 'own' his toys. He has fun playing and interacting with you, but the game is over – and the toy is given up – when you say so.

- If your Shih Tzu has been guarding his food bowl, put the bowl down empty and drop in a little food at a time. Periodically stop dropping in the food and tell your Shih Tzu to "Sit" and "Wait". Give it a few seconds and then reward him by dropping in more food. This shows your Shih Tzu that you are the provider of the food and he can only eat when you allow him to.

- Make sure the family eats before you feed your Shih Tzu. Some trainers advocate eating in front of the dog (maybe just a few bites from a biscuit) before starting a training session, so the dog appreciates your elevated status.

- Do not let your Shih Tzu run through doors ahead of you or leap from the back of the car before you release him. You may need to put your dog on the lead and teach him to "Wait" at doorways, or in the back of the car, and then reward him when you have given the release command.

If your Shih Tzu is progressing well with his retraining programme, think about giving him additional stimulation by joining a training club, or maybe having a go at a dog sport, such as agility. This will give your Shih Tzu a positive outlet for his energies. However, if your Shih Tzu is still seeking to be assertive, or you have any other concerns, do not delay in seeking the help of an animal behaviourist.

SEPARATION ANXIETY

A Shih Tzu should be brought up to accept short periods of separation from his owner so that he does not become anxious. This is important with a breed that thrives on being with people. A new puppy should be left for

A Shih Tzu would much rather be with his beloved owners than home alone.

short periods on his own, ideally in a crate where he cannot get up to any mischief. It is a good idea to leave him with a boredom-busting toy so he will be happily occupied in your absence. When you return, do not rush to the crate and make a huge fuss. Wait a few minutes, and then calmly go to the crate and release your dog, telling him how good he has been. If this scenario is repeated a number of times, your Shih Tzu will soon learn that being left on his own is no big deal.

Problems with separation anxiety are most likely to arise if you take on a rescued dog who has major insecurities. You may also find that your Shih Tzu hates being left if you have failed to accustom him to short periods of isolation when he was growing up. Separation anxiety is expressed in a number of ways and all are equally distressing for both dog and owner. An anxious dog who is left alone may bark and whine continuously, urinate and defecate, and may be extremely destructive. There are a number of steps you can take when attempting to solve this problem.

- Put up a baby-gate between adjoining rooms and leave your dog in one room while you are in the other room. Your dog will be able to see you and hear you, but he is learning to cope without being right next to you. Build up the amount of time you can leave your dog in easy stages.

- Buy some boredom-busting toys and fill them with some tasty treats. Whenever you leave your dog, give him a food-filled toy so that he is busy while you are away.
- If you have not used a crate before, it is not too late to start. Make sure the crate is cosy and train your Shih Tzu to get used to going in his crate while you are in the same room. Gradually build up the amount of time he spends in the crate and then start leaving the room for short periods. When you return, do not make a fuss of your dog. Leave him for five or ten minutes before releasing him, so that he gets used to your comings and goings.

- Pretend to go out, putting on your coat and jangling keys, but do not leave the house. An anxious dog often becomes hyped up by the ritual of leaving and this will help to desensitize him.
- When you go out, leave a radio or a TV on. Some dogs are comforted by hearing voices and background noise

AGGRESSION

Aggression is a complex issue, as there are different causes and the behaviour may be triggered by numerous factors. It may be directed towards people, but far more commonly it is directed towards other dogs. Aggression in dogs may be the result of:

- Assertive behaviour (see page 105).
- Defensive behaviour: This may be induced by fear, pain or punishment.
- Territory: A dog may become aggressive if strange dogs or people enter his territory (which is generally seen as the house and garden).
- Intra-sexual issues: This is aggression between sexes – male-to-male or female-to-female.
- Parental instinct: A mother dog may become aggressive if she is protecting her puppies.

The Shih Tzu is an outgoing, friendly dog, and rarely has problems relating to other dogs. If you allow your puppy to mix with other dogs of sound temperament from an early age, it will help him to learn good canine manners that other dogs will understand.

However, you may have taken on an older, rescued dog that has been poorly socialised and may have experienced something in his history that has made him aggressive. Or you may have a dog who has become dominant in his own home and family and so he is assertive in his dealings with other dogs. This sometimes happens if you are keeping a number of dogs and one decides he wants to take on the role of top dog.

If dominance is the underlying cause, you can try the measures outlined in this chapter. If your dog has been poorly socialised, you can try to make up for lost time and work with other dogs of sound temperament in controlled situations. But if you are concerned about your dog's behaviour, you would be well advised to call in professional help. If the aggression is directed towards people, you should seek immediate advice. This behaviour can escalate very quickly and could lead to disastrous consequences.

when they are left alone.
• Try to make your absences as short as possible when you are first training your dog to accept being on his own.

If you take these steps, your dog should become less anxious, and, over a period of time, you should be able to solve the problem. However, if you are failing to make progress, do not delay in calling in expert help.

NEW CHALLENGES

If you enjoy training your Shih Tzu, you may want to try one of the many dog sports that are now on offer. Obviously, the Shih Tzu will not be able to participate in the sports designed for bigger dogs, but you will be surprised by what you can achieve with a well-trained Shih Tzu.

GOOD CITIZEN SCHEME

This is a scheme run by the Kennel Club in the UK and the American Kennel Club in the USA. The schemes promote responsible ownership and help you to train a well-behaved dog who will fit in with the community. The schemes are excellent for all pet owners and they are also a good starting point if you plan to compete with your Shih Tzu when he is older. The KC and the AKC schemes vary in format. In the UK there are three levels: bronze, silver and gold, with each test becoming

Why not have a go at one of the canine sports on offer?

progressively more demanding. In the AKC scheme there is a single test.

Some of the exercises include:
• Walking on a loose lead among people and other dogs.
• Recall amid distractions.
• A controlled greeting where dogs stay under control while their owners meet.
• The dog allows all-over grooming and handling by his owner, and also accepts being handled by the examiner.
• Stays, with the owner in sight and then out of sight.
• Food manners, allowing the owner to eat without begging and taking a treat on command.
• Sendaway – sending the dog to his bed.

The tests are designed to show the control you have over your dog and his ability to respond correctly and remain calm in all situations. The Good Citizen Scheme is taught at most training clubs. For more information, log on to the Kennel Club or AKC website (see Appendices).

SHOWING

In your eyes, your Shih Tzu is the most beautiful dog in the world – but would a judge agree? Showing is a highly competitive sport, and, at the top level, presentation is all important. However, many owners get bitten by the showing bug, and their calendar is governed by the dates of the top showing fixtures.

To be successful in the show ring, a Shih Tzu must conform as closely as possible to the Breed Standard, which is a written blueprint describing the 'perfect' Shih Tzu (see Chapter Seven), and he must be groomed to a very high standard so he looks his very best in the ring.

To get started you need to buy a puppy that has show potential and then train him to perform in the ring. A Shih Tzu will be expected to stand in show pose, gait for the judge in order to show off his natural movement, and to be examined by the judge. This involves a detailed hands-on examination, so your Shih Tzu must be bombproof when handled by strangers.

Many training clubs hold ringcraft classes, which are run by experienced showgoers. At these classes, you will learn how to handle your Shih Tzu in the ring, and you will also find out about rules, procedures and show-ring etiquette.

The best plan is to start off at some small, informal shows where you can practise and learn the tricks of the trade before graduating to bigger shows. It's a long haul starting in the very first puppy class, but the dream is to make your Shih Tzu a Champion.

Showing can be very rewarding – but you need to have plenty of time to perfect your Shih Tzu's show presentation.

COMPETITIVE OBEDIENCE

In the UK, this sport is dominated by Border Collies, German Shepherd Dogs and some of the Gundog breeds. However, in other countries – particularly in the USA – owners of other breeds, including those with small dogs, are keen to have a go and many achieve a fair degree of success. The classes start off at beginner level and become increasingly complex as dog and handler become more advanced. The exercises that must be mastered include the following:

- **Heelwork:** Dog and handler must complete a set pattern on and off the lead, which includes left turns, right turns, about turns and changes of pace.
- **Recall:** This may be when the handler is stationary or on the move.
- **Retrieve:** This may be a dumbbell or any article chosen by the judge.
- **Sendaway:** The dog is sent to a designated spot and must go into an instant 'Down' until he is recalled by the handler.
- **Stays:** The dog must stay in the 'Sit' and in the 'Down' for a set amount of time. In advanced classes, the handler is out of sight.
- **Scent:** The dog must retrieve a single cloth from a pre-arranged pattern of cloths that has his owner's scent, or, in advanced classes, the judge's scent. There may also be decoy cloths.
- **Distance control.** The dog must execute a series of exercises ('Sit', 'Stand', 'Down') without moving from his position and with the handler at a distance.

Even though competitive obedience requires accuracy and precision, make sure it is fun for your Shih Tzu, with lots of praise and rewards so that you motivate him to do his best. Many training clubs run advanced classes for those who want to compete in obedience, or you can hire the services of a professional trainer for one-on-one sessions.

You may decide to have a go at Rally O, which is a relatively new sport, developed in the USA. In this, dogs compete in a variety of exercises, going from stage to stage, until the finish when points are calculated. The exercises are more varied than in competitive obedience, and accuracy is not of such paramount importance.

AGILITY

This fun sport has grown enormously in popularity over the past few years, and the Shih Tzu is perfectly capable of competing in the classes for small dogs.

In agility competitions, each dog must complete a set course over a series of obstacles, which include:

- Jumps (upright hurdles and long jump, varying in height – small, medium and large, depending on the size of the dog)
- Weaves
- A-frame
- Dog walk
- Seesaw
- Tunnels (collapsible and rigid)
- Tyre

Whatever discipline you compete in, remember, you always take the best dog home with you.

Dogs may compete in Jumping classes, with jumps, tunnels and weaves, or in Agility classes, which have the full set of equipment. Faults are awarded for poles down on the jumps, missed contact points on the A-frame, dog walk and seesaw, and refusals. If a dog takes the wrong course, he is eliminated. The winner is the dog that completes the course in the fastest time with no faults. As you progress up the levels, courses become progressively harder with more twists, turns and changes of direction.

If you want to get involved in agility, you will need to find a club that specialises in the sport (see Appendices). You will not be allowed to start training until your Shih Tzu is 12 months old and you cannot compete until he is 18 months old. This rule is for the protection of the dog, who may suffer injury if he puts strain on bones and joints while he is still growing.

SUMMING UP

The Shih Tzu is one of the most charming of all breeds – he is intelligent, watchful, full of fun and immensely loving and loyal. Make sure you keep your half of the bargain: spend time socialising and training your Shih Tzu so you establish a mutual sense of trust and respect, and you will have a dog that you can take anywhere and that will always be a credit to you.

THE PERFECT SHIH TZU

Chapter 7

Has there ever really been a 'perfect Shih Tzu'? I think not. Indeed, there have been several who have come close to perfection, but the really genuine, experienced dog breeder or exhibitor will always acknowledge that there is just that tiny 'something' that could be little touch better.

In truth, there is no perfect dog in any breed; nonetheless, perfection is what all good breeders strive for and to do this they aim to breed dogs that adhere as closely as possible to the Breed Standard.

WHAT IS A BREED STANDARD?

A Breed Standard is effectively a picture of a breed, painted in words, but, of course, everyone will interpret a picture slightly differently. So it is with people's perception of dogs and the way in which a Standard is interpreted. If we all viewed Shih Tzu in the very same way, it would always be the same dog who won at shows, and this is certainly not the case.

Each breeder and every judge puts emphasis on certain traits that they consider the most important, although of course every dog must be assessed as a whole. Added to this a breed specialist will often look for slightly different breed attributes than does an all-rounder (someone who judges many different breeds), but basically we are all aiming to breed and possibly to judge dogs that most closely meet the Standard as set down by the national kennel club. Breeding with the Breed Standard closely in our mind's eye means that we are aiming to breed a Shih Tzu as opposed to any other breed of dog, for each breed's Standard is different.

Breed Standards vary slightly from country to country. The FCI (Fédération Cynologique Internationale or International Canine Federation) is an umbrella organisation for many European and some South American countries. It usually adheres to the Breed Standard of each breed's country of origin.

Essentially, all the Breed Standards are roughly the same, but there are slight differences, such as the wording regarding size, which differs in the USA from the UK and FCI Standards. Also in the US Standard, specific faults are included, which they are not in the other two Standards. Another important difference between the three Standards is that the bite is to be undershot in the US, whereas in the English and FCI Standards it

Ch. Tameron Mr XS: A leading British Shih Tzu, winner of 28 Challenge Certificates (19 with Best of Breed) and 16 Reserve CCs.
Photo courtesy Carol Ann Johnson.

Am Ch. Lou Wan Rebel Rouser: Sire of more than 136 Champioms in the USA.

Multi Ch. Fosella Kama Sutra has won Best in Show three times at Sweden's prestigious Tibethund Show.

HEALTH AND FITNESS FOR PURPOSE

In January 2009, the English Kennel Club revised its Breed Standards and introduced the following clause that is worthy of note: *"A Breed Standard is the guideline which describes the ideal characteristics, temperament and appearance of a breed and ensures that the breed is fit for function. Absolute soundness is essential. Breeders and judges should at all times be careful to avoid obvious conditions or exaggerations which would be detrimental in any way to the health, welfare or soundness of this breed.*

"From time to time, certain conditions or exaggerations may be considered to have the potential to affect dogs in some breeds adversely, and judges and breeders are requested to refer to the Kennel Club website for details of any such current issues. If a feature or quality is desirable it should only be present in the right measure."

is to be slightly undershot, or level.

The Standards are also laid out in slightly different ways, with different sub-headings, added to which the English Kennel Club has adapted the Standard a little to tie in with its recent policy of 'Fitness For Purpose'.

ANALYSIS AND INTERPRETATION

UK
GENERAL APPEARANCE
Sturdy, abundantly but not excessively coated dog with distinctly arrogant carriage and 'chrysanthemum-like' face.

CHARACTERISTICS
Intelligent, active and alert.

TEMPERAMENT
Friendly and independent.

The Shih Tzu is a sturdy little dog with a distinct air of arrogance.

SHIH TZU

USA
GENERAL APPEARANCE
The Shih Tzu is a sturdy, lively, alert toy dog with long flowing double coat. Befitting his noble Chinese ancestry as a highly valued, prized companion and palace pet, the Shih Tzu is proud of bearing, has a distinctively arrogant carriage with head well up and tail curved over the back. Although there has always been considerable size variation, the Shih Tzu must be compact, solid, carrying good weight and substance.

Even though a toy dog, the Shih Tzu must be subject to the same requirements of soundness and structure prescribed for all breeds, and any deviation from the ideal described in the standard should be penalized to the extent of the deviation. Structural faults common to all breeds are as undesirable in the Shih Tzu as in any other breed, regardless of whether or not such faults are specifically mentioned in the standard.

The chrysanthemum-like effect to the face is a hallmark of the breed.

TEMPERAMENT
As the sole purpose of the Shih Tzu is that of a companion and house pet, it is essential that its temperament be outgoing, happy, affectionate, friendly and trusting towards all.

FCI
GENERAL APPEARANCE
Sturdy, abundantly coated dog with distinctly arrogant carriage and chrysanthemum-like face.

BEHAVIOUR/TEMPERAMENT
Intelligent, active and alert. Friendly and independent.

Under 'General Appearance', a picture is conjured up of a sturdy, abundantly coated dog that has a distinctly arrogant carriage. The US Standard goes into greater detail, but much of this is incorporated in other specific sections.

From 'Characteristics' and 'Temperament' we learn a lot about the Shih Tzu's personality in words that speak for themselves.

UK
HEAD AND SKULL
Head broad, round, wide between eyes. Shock-headed with hair falling well over eyes, not affecting the dog's ability to see. Good beard and whiskers, hair growing upwards on the muzzle giving a distinctly 'chrysanthemum-like' effect. Muzzle of ample width, square, short, not wrinkled; flat and hairy. Nose black but dark liver in liver or liver marked dogs

Viewed in profile, the stop is steep and the length of nose is about one inch (2.5 cm) from tip to stop.

An American Shih Tzu ready for the show ring (note the difference in presentation).

and about one inch from tip to definite stop. Nose level or slightly tip-tilted. Top of nose leather should be on a line with or slightly below lower eye-rim. Wide-open nostrils. Down-pointed nose highly undesirable, as are pinched nostrils. Pigmentation of muzzle as unbroken as possible.

EYES

Large, dark, round, placed well apart but not prominent. Warm expression. In liver or liver-marked dogs, lighter eye colour permissible. No white of eye showing.

EARS

Large, with long leathers, carried drooping. Set slightly below crown of skull, so heavily coated they appear to blend into hair of neck.

MOUTH

Wide, slightly undershot or level. Lips level.

USA

HEAD

Head – Round, broad, wide between eyes, its size in balance with the overall size of dog being neither too large nor too small. Fault: Narrow head, close-set eyes. *Expression* – Warm, sweet, wide-eyed, friendly and trusting. An overall well-balanced and pleasant expression supersedes the importance of individual parts. Care should be taken to look and examine well beyond the hair to determine if what is seen is the actual head and expression rather than an image created by grooming technique.

Eyes – Large, round, not prominent, placed well apart, looking straight ahead. Very dark. Lighter on liver pigmented dogs and blue pigmented dogs. Fault: Small,

close-set or light eyes; excessive eye white.

Ears – Large, set slightly below crown of skull; heavily coated.

Skull – Domed.

Stop – There is a definite stop.

Muzzle – Square, short, unwrinkled, with good cushioning, set no lower than bottom eye rim; never downturned. Ideally, no longer than 1 inch from tip of nose to stop, although length may vary slightly in relation to overall size of dog. Front of muzzle should be flat; lower lip and chin not protruding and definitely never receding. Fault: Snipiness, lack of definite stop.

Nose – Nostrils are broad, wide, and open.

Pigmentation – Nose, lips, eye rims are black on all colors, except liver on liver pigmented dogs and blue on blue pigmented dogs. Fault: Pink

on nose, lips, or eye rims.
Bite – Undershot. Jaw is
broad and wide. A missing
tooth or slightly misaligned
teeth should not be too
severely penalized. Teeth and
tongue should not show when
mouth is closed. Fault:
Overshot bite.

FCI
HEAD
Head broad, round, wide
between the eyes. Shock-
headed with hair falling well
over eyes. Good beard and
whiskers, hair growing upwards
on the nose giving a distinctly
chrysanthemum-like effect.

CRANIAL REGION
Stop: Definite.

FACIAL REGION
Nose: Black but dark liver in
liver or liver marked dogs. Top
of nose leather should be on a
line with or slightly below
lower eye rim. Down-pointed
nose highly undesirable. Wide
open nostrils. Pinched nostrils
highly undesirable.
Muzzle: Of ample width,
square, short, not wrinkled, flat
and hairy. Length about one
inch (2.5 cm) from tip to stop.
Bridge of the nose level or
slightly tip tilted. Pigmentation
of muzzle as unbroken as
possible.
Lips: Level.
Jaws/Teeth: Wide, slightly
undershot or level.
Eyes: Large, dark, round,
placed well apart but not
prominent. Warm expression.

The bite may be slightly undershot or level.

In liver or liver marked dogs,
lighter eye colour permissible.
No white of eye showing.
Ears: Large, with long leathers,
carried drooping. Set slightly
below crown of skull, so
heavily coated they appear to
blend into hair of neck.

The skull shape of the Shih Tzu
is a characteristic feature of the
breed and, if correct, it is quite
different from those of its
ancestors – the Pekingese and the
Lhasa Apso. The Shih Tzu's skull
falls somewhere in the middle of
the two. It is broader than that of
the Lhasa Apso, but not so flat as
the Pekingese. In keeping with
the shape of the skull, the eye
shape is correspondingly different
too; less prominent than that of
the Pekingese, but more so than
in the Lhasa Apso, and the Shih
Tzu has a greater width between
the eyes than the latter.

Although the US Standard only
penalises excessive eye white, the
other Standards ask for no white

of eye. Certainly we do not
require too large an eye, which
would be out of proportion with
the size of the head.

When we look at the Shih Tzu
from head on, we see that the
top of the nose is either in line
with, or slightly below, the lower
eye rim; it may be just slightly
tilted upward but should
certainly not be down-pointed.

As you look at the head in
profile, the steep stop is clearly
evident and you will see the
correct angle of the nose. The
length from tip of nose to stop
versus stop to occiput is roughly
as 1 is to 4 (or 5). It is important
that the length of nose is in
proportion to the size of the
head, and, indeed, the head must
be in balance with the body.

Nostrils should never be
pinched, as we do not wish to
encourage this problem in the Shih
Tzu. Pigment should always be
black, except in certain colours as
outlined in the Breed Standards.

Chin is desirable, but not too
much of it. The actual strength,
breadth and depth of chin are
usually dependent upon the
placement of the jaw and teeth.
For example, a Shih Tzu with a
scissor bite is much more likely
to lack underjaw; conversely, a
heavily undershot dog will appear
too strong in underjaw. When the
mouth is closed, the teeth should
not show and the upper lip
should close over the lower.

This is one of the few breeds in
which complete dentition is not
called for in the Standard, but
clearly, in an ideal situation, six
incisors in both the upper and

Assessing conformation in a heavily coated breed is no easy matter, and the judge requires a hands-on examination. Here, we can take a look at a dog in pet trim to get a better idea of construction.

lower jaws are preferable. In order to achieve the desired width of jaw, they should be evenly placed. Having said that, the Standards are quite lenient regarding the mouth of the Shih Tzu. As in any breed, a wry mouth is to be avoided.

The head of the male Shih Tzu should be somewhat larger and more masculine than that of a bitch, which should have a distinctly feminine expression. In essence, you should be able to look at a dog and know he is a male, and vice versa. Ears are set on below the crown, not so high as on the Pekingese.

The American Standard wisely incorporates the comment that care should be taken to look well beyond the hair; this is highly relevant, as clever hairdressing can camouflage a multitude of sins. It is also worth pointing out that now, in many countries other than the UK, Shih Tzu's top-knots are taken to the

extreme, which, in my personal opinion makes the breed look more like an over-exaggerated childhood beauty idol! What a great pity that is.

UK
NECK
Well proportioned, nicely arched. Sufficient length to carry head proudly.

FOREQUARTERS
Shoulders well laid back. Legs short and muscular with ample bone, as straight as possible, consistent with broad chest being well let down.

BODY
Longer between withers and root of tail than height of withers, well coupled and sturdy, chest broad and deep, shoulders firm, back level.

HINDQUARTERS
Legs short and muscular with

ample bone. Straight when viewed from the rear. Thighs well rounded and muscular.

FEET
Rounded, firm and well covered with hair.

USA
NECK, TOPLINE, BODY
Of utmost importance is an overall well-balanced dog with no exaggerated features.
Neck – Well set-on flowing smoothly into shoulders; of sufficient length to permit natural high head carriage and in balance with height and length of dog.
Topline – Level.
Body – Short-coupled and sturdy with no waist or tuck-up. The Shih Tzu is slightly longer than tall. Fault: Legginess.
Chest – Broad and deep with good spring-of-rib, however, not barrel-chested. Depth of ribcage

FRONT CONSTRUCTION

The chest is broad and the legs are short and muscular.

should extend to just below elbow. Distance from elbow to withers is a little greater than from elbow to ground.
Croup – Flat.
Tail – Set on high, heavily plumed, carried in curve well over back. Too loose, too tight, too flat, or too low set a tail is undesirable and should be penalized to extent of deviation.

FOREQUARTERS
Shoulders –Well-angulated, well laid-back, well laid-in, fitting smoothly into body.
Legs – Straight, well-boned, muscular, set well-apart and under chest, with elbows set close to body.

Pasterns – Strong, perpendicular.
Dewclaws – May be removed.
Feet – Firm, well-padded, point straight ahead.

HINDQUARTERS
Angulation of hindquarters should be in balance with forequarters.
Legs –Well-boned, muscular, and straight when viewed from rear with well-bent stifles, not close set but in line with forequarters.
Hocks – Well let down, perpendicular. Fault: Hyperextension of hocks.
Dewclaws – May be removed.
Feet – Firm, well-padded, point straight ahead.

FCI
NECK
Well proportioned, nicely arched. Sufficient length to carry head proudly.

BODY
Longer between withers and root of the tail than height at withers.
Back: Level.
Loin: Well coupled and sturdy.
Chest: Broad and deep.

FOREQUARTERS
Legs short and muscular with ample bone, as straight as possible, consistent with broad chest being well let down.
Shoulders: Firm, well laid back.

HINDQUARTERS
Legs short and muscular with ample bone. Straight when viewed from the rear. Legs looking massive on account of wealth of hair.
Thighs: Well rounded and muscular.

FEET
Rounded, firm and well padded, appearing big on account of wealth of hair.

It is important to assess a Shih Tzu's neck and forequarters together, for one has a bearing on the other. A dog that is too upright in shoulder is likely to appear too short in the neck, for the withers are further forward resulting in a 'stuffy' appearance. A well-proportioned neck should be of sufficient length to carry the head proudly, but it should not be over-long for that would destroy the balance of the dog. Coat can hide certain faults, but a good judge can easily discover constructional faults in the forehand assembly, not only on the table but also on the move.

Because of the height of the Shih Tzu and the shape of his ribcage, it would be impossible to have completely straight front legs, such as those of a terrier. The UK and FCI Standards wisely ask for them to be "as straight as possible", while the American Standard asks for them to be "straight", something that is difficult to achieve as the Shih Tzu has a broad chest which is well let down. The legs, however, should certainly be straight enough to allow the feet to point straight forward; they should turn neither in nor out.

There is also a difference in the description of bone, the UK and FCI Standards asking for "ample bone", while the in the USA the requirement is for them to be "well boned". I have seen Shih Tzu in the UK with too much bone and, while I appreciate that this is a sturdy breed, when bone is too heavy I feel this completely spoils the dog.

The withers are located at the uppermost point of the scapulae and the Shih Tzu is longer between withers and root of tail than the height from ground to withers. But we should not be looking for extreme length, as this is a sturdy, well coupled dog, with a reasonably short coupling (the length is in the back).

REAR CONSTRUCTION

The angulation of the hindquarters should be in balance with the forequarters. *Photo © Carol Ann Johnson.*

Looking at a Shih Tzu in profile, we should be able to 'see' an imaginary perpendicular line running from the rearmost point of the scapula through the back of the elbow. Also the upper arm should not be too short or the Shih Tzu will lack the facility of forehand extension.

The chest should be broad and deep, reaching to very slightly below the elbow, but a true barrel chest is not called for, as this is more akin to the Pekingese. The underline of the Shih Tzu should be virtually parallel with the line of the back, which is level; any accentuated tuck-up at the loin would be untypical. There should be no roach on the back.

Shoulders are firm, but not loaded; the muscle should be in hard condition, contributing to the sturdiness that is required in the Breed Standard.

The hindlegs are short, to maintain balance with the front ones, and this is another area of the assembly in which we should look for muscle. They should be straight when viewed from the rear, meaning there should be no bowing out or any cow hocks. The word 'straight' definitely does not indicate the Shih Tzu should be straight in stifle, which would give a more stilted action than is required for the Shih Tzu. The Americans have taken the trouble to point out that the "Angulation of the hindquarters should be in balance with the forequarters", something that is hopefully taken as read when reading the other two Standards. Thighs should be well rounded.

Like the forefeet, the hind feet should point neither in nor out, but straight forward. All feet should be rounded, firm and well padded. Because they are so well covered with hair, they look larger than they actually are.

UK
TAIL
Heavily plumed, carried gaily well over back. Set on high. Height approximately level with that of skull to give a balanced outline.

USA
TAIL
Set on high, heavily plumed, carried in curve well over back.

Too loose, too tight, too flat, or too low set a tail is undesirable and should be penalized to extent of deviation.

FCI
TAIL
Heavily plumed carried gaily well over back. Set on high. Height approximately level with that of skull to give a balanced outline.

In a long-coated breed like the Shih Tzu, the abundantly furnished tail can be used to hide faulty construction, such as a roached back. Hopefully, judges will see through this deception and not simply judge on the basis of the picture presented by the exhibitor when the dog is standing in profile. I feel strongly that breeders should endeavour

to breed out constructional faults, not simply grow coat to hide them.

The Shih Tzu's high-set tail should be in balance with the head, so those that lie flat, or which are too low set are uncharacteristic. It should be carried like a pot handle, or as accurately described in the US Standard "in a curve well over the back". It must not, though, be too tightly curled, as this will spoil the balance of the outline. A tail when well feathered puts the finishing touch to the Shih Tzu's highly attractive overall picture.

UK
GAIT/MOVEMENT
Arrogant, smooth-flowing, front legs reaching well forward, strong rear action and showing full pad.

USA
GAIT
The Shih Tzu moves straight and must be shown at its own natural speed, neither raced nor strung-up, to evaluate its smooth, flowing, effortless movement with good front reach and equally strong rear drive, level topline, naturally high head carriage, and tail carried in gentle curve over back.

FCI
GAIT / MOVEMENT
Arrogant, smooth-flowing, front legs reaching well forward, strong rear action and showing full pad.

The tail is carried well over the back.

ON THE MOVE

A dog that is put together correctly will move correctly.

The rear action is strong, and the full pad should be visible when watching from behind.

The front legs should reach well forward and this must, of necessity, be coupled with a strong rear action, which shows the full pad when watching the movement from behind. Movement is smooth-flowing, often likened to a ship in full sail; the arrogance of the Shih Tzu is displayed in his movement.

If the neck and head carriage are correct, the dog should be able to move with his head held high, without the necessity to string him up by his lead. The Shih Tzu should be moved at a steady pace by the exhibitor and not at great speed as, unfortunately, one sees happen too frequently. The American Standard actually says the Shih Tzu should be "neither raced nor strung up". A correctly assembled, well-balanced Shih Tzu moves smoothly and with head and tail held high; and when in full coat this is a veritable joy to watch.

UK
COAT

Long, dense, not curly, with good undercoat. Slight wave permitted. Strongly recommended that hair on head tied up. Hair not affecting the dog's ability to see.

COLOUR

All colours permissible, white blaze on forehead and white tip to tail highly desirable in parti-colours.

USA
COAT

Coat – Luxurious, double-coated, dense, long, and flowing. Slight wave permissible. Hair on top of head is tied up. Fault: Sparse coat, single coat, curly coat. *Trimming* – Feet, bottom of coat, and anus may be done for neatness and to facilitate movement. Fault: Excessive trimming.

The coat is shown in its full glory when Shih Tzu are exhibited in the ring.

COLOR AND MARKINGS
All are permissible and to be considered *equally*.

FCI
HAIR
Long, dense not curly, with good undercoat. Slight wave permitted. Strongly recommended that hair on head tied up.

COLOUR
All colours permissible, white blaze on forehead and white tip to tail highly desirable in parti-colours.

The Shih Tzu's coat is long, with a good undercoat; a slight wave is permitted, though not a curly one. None of the Standards mention texture of coat, and, in fact, this varies rather, depending upon colour. Head hair is tied up in a top-knot and there should be ample furnishings on the tail and ears, and plenty of coat on the feet.

All colours are permissible in the Shih Tzu. This includes colours that are genetically liver and in which the pigment is of corresponding colour. In the UK and FCI Breed Standards, a white blaze on the forehead and white tip to the tail are highly desirable in particolours, but the US Standard stresses that all colours are to be considered equally.

There are not a great many black Shih Tzu in the show ring, but in this colour judges should be aware that it is less easy to see the detail of expression. It is therefore important that judges 'see' with their hands, as well as their eyes.

UK
SIZE
Height at withers not more than 27 cms (10$\frac{1}{2}$ ins), type and breed characteristics of the utmost importance and on no account to be sacrificed to size alone. Weight: 4.5-8 kgs (10-18

lbs). Ideal weight 4.5-7.5 kgs (10-16 lbs).

USA
SIZE, PROPORTION, SUBSTANCE

Size – Ideally, height at withers is 9 to 10$\frac{1}{2}$ inches; but, not less than 8 inches nor more than 11 inches. Ideally, weight of mature dogs, 9 to 16 pounds.
Proportion – Length between withers and root of tail is slightly longer than height at withers. *The Shih Tzu must never be so high stationed as to appear leggy, nor so low stationed as to appear dumpy or squatty.*
Substance – Regardless of size, the Shih Tzu is always compact, solid and carries good weight and substance.

FCI
SIZE AND WEIGHT

Height at the withers: Not more than 26.7 cms (10$\frac{1}{2}$ ins), type and breed characteristics of the utmost importance and on no account to be sacrificed to size alone.
Weight: 4.5 to 8.1 kgs (10-18 lbs). Ideal weight 4.5-7.3 kgs (10-16 lbs).

The Shih Tzu is heavy for his size and those who are not familiar with the breed can be in for quite a shock when they pick one up. The weight range is enormously wide for a small dog, and it is the breed's history that has had a bearing on this. As you will read in the extracts from the various Standards above, ideal weights are given, and the lower limit is slightly less in America. But the UK and FCI Standards allow a weight up to almost a kilo more than that which is considered ideal.

Regarding height, there is also some difference between the UK and FCI Standards and that for the USA. In the first two, the height at withers should be not more than 26.7 kg (10$\frac{1}{2}$ ins), with the additional clause that on no account should breed type be sacrificed to size alone. However, the American Standard gives an ideal height of 9 to 10$\frac{1}{2}$ inches, also allowing for a wider range of 8 to 11 inches. The clause in the US Standard which reads: "Regardless of size, the Shih Tzu is always compact, solid and carries good weight and substance'" speaks volumes.

UK
FAULTS

Any departure from the foregoing points should be considered a fault and the seriousness with which the fault should be regarded should be in exact proportion to its degree and its effect upon the health and welfare of the dog.

NOTE

Male animals should have two apparently normal testicles fully descended into the scrotum.

USA

Individual faults are listed in the various sections, as incorporated above.

FCI
FAULTS

Any departure from the foregoing points should be considered a fault and the seriousness with which the fault should be regarded should be in exact proportion to its degree and its effect upon the health and welfare of the dog.

The Shih Tzu is surprisingly heavy for his size.

It is the dog who, in the judge's opinion, conforms most closely to the Breed Standard that will win on the day.

Any dog clearly showing physical or behavioural abnormalities shall be disqualified.

N.B.
Male animals should have two apparently normal testicles fully descended into the scrotum.

In no British Standard are faults listed individually as they used to be decades ago, but instead all deviations from the Standards are considered a fault, and the seriousness with which they should be regarded is to be in proportion not only to its degree but now also its effect upon the health and welfare of the dog.

All males should have two apparently normal testicles fully descended into the scrotum, and if this is not the case exhibitors should be able to provide the judge with a veterinary letter explaining that an operation has taken place, and why.

The USA Standard treats the matter in a different way, and, as you read through each section of the Standard as outlined above, you will see specific faults listed, one of which is 'Excessive trimming', which I am delighted to see.

Take every opportunity to learn as much as you can about this fascinating breed.

SUMMING UP

The Shih Tzu Breed Standard gives a reasonably clear outline of the breed, but it is very important for breeders, judges, exhibitors and other enthusiasts to realise that reading a Standard alone is not sufficient to understand the breed fully. It is essential to talk about the Shih Tzu with as many knowledgeable people as you can;

maybe some of them will even allow you to go over their dogs in a quiet place, enabling you to assess their virtues, and, if you are really lucky, their faults, too.

Go along to any seminars that are on offer for the breed, even if it means travelling some distance and perhaps foregoing a show or two. There will be a great deal you can learn from the ringside,

but, in a coated breed, 'hands on' experience is essential.

The Shih Tzu is a truly wonderful breed, both in personality and in looks. So if you really want to do the breed justice, explore every avenue to learn all you can about it. In this way you will not be disappointed, nor will you disappoint the breed.

HAPPY AND HEALTHY

Chapter 8

hih Tzus are stoical dogs with a life span that can run well into double figures. The Shih Tzu is renowned as a faithful companion and a willing friend on a non-conditional basis. He will, however, of necessity rely on you for food and shelter, accident prevention and medication. A healthy Shih Tzu is a happy chap, looking to please and amuse his owner.

There are very few genetic conditions recognised in the Shih Tzu, which will be covered in depth later in the chapter.

VACCINATION

There is much debate over the issue of vaccination at the moment. The timing of the final part of the initial vaccination course for a puppy, and the frequency of subsequent booster vaccinations, are both under scrutiny. An evaluation of the relative risk for each disease plays a part, depending on the local situation.

Many owners think that the actual vaccination is the protection, so that their puppy can go out for walks as soon as he or she has had the final part of the puppy vaccination course. This is not the case. The rationale behind vaccination is to stimulate the immune system into producing protective antibodies, which will be triggered if the patient is subsequently exposed to that particular disease. This means that a further one or two weeks will have to pass before an effective level of protection will have developed.

Vaccines against viruses stimulate longer-lasting protection than those against bacteria, whose effect may only persist for a matter of months in some cases. There is also the possibility of an individual failing to mount a full immune response to a vaccination: although the vaccine schedule may have been followed as recommended, that particular dog remains vulnerable.

A dog's level of protection against rabies, as demonstrated by the antibody titre in a blood sample, is routinely tested in the UK in order to fulfil the requirements of the Pet Travel Scheme (PETS). This is not required at the current time with any other individual diseases in order to gauge the need for booster vaccination or to determine the effect of a course of vaccines; instead, your veterinary surgeon will advise a protocol based upon the vaccines available, local disease prevalence, and the lifestyle of you and your dog.

It is worth remembering that maintaining a fully effective level of immune protection against the disease appropriate to your locale

A puppy receives first immunity from his mother's milk.

is vital: these are serious diseases, which may result in the death of your dog, and some may have the potential to be passed on to his human family (so-called zoonotic potential for transmission). This is where you will be grateful for your veterinary surgeon's own knowledge and advice.

The American Animal Hospital Association laid down guidance at the end of 2006 for the vaccination of dogs in North America. Core diseases were defined as distemper, adenovirus, parvovirus and rabies. So-called non-core diseases are kennel cough, Lyme disease and leptospirosis. A decision to vaccinate against one or more non-core diseases will be based on an individual's level of risk, determined on lifestyle and where you live in the US.

Do remember, however, that the booster visit to the veterinary surgery is not 'just' for a booster. I am regularly correcting my clients when they announce that they have 'just' brought their pet for a booster. Instead, this appointment is a chance for a full health check and evaluation of how a particular dog is doing. After all, we are all conversant with the adage that a human year is equivalent to seven canine years.

There have been attempts in recent times to reset the scale for two reasons: small breeds live longer than giant breeds, and dogs are living longer than previously. I have seen dogs of 17 and 18 years of age, but to say a dog is 119 or 126 years old is plainly meaningless. It does emphasise the fact, though, that a dog's health can change dramatically over the course of a single year, because dogs age at a far faster rate than humans.

For me as a veterinary surgeon, the booster vaccination visit is a challenge: how much can I find of which the owner was unaware, such as rotten teeth or a heart murmur? Even monitoring bodyweight year upon year is of use, because bodyweight can creep up, or down, without an owner realising. Being overweight is unhealthy, but it may take an outsider's remark to make an owner realise that there is a problem. Conversely, a drop in bodyweight may be the only pointer to an underlying problem.

The diseases against which dogs are vaccinated include:

ADENOVIRUS
Canine adenovirus 1 (CAV-1) affects the liver (hepatitis) and is seen within affected dogs as the classic 'blue eye', while CAV-2 is a cause of kennel cough (see later). Vaccines often include both canine adenoviruses.

DISTEMPER
This disease is sometimes called 'hardpad' from the characteristic changes to the pads of the paws.

It has a worldwide distribution, but fortunately vaccination has been very effective at reducing its occurrence. It is caused by a virus and affects the respiratory, gastro-intestinal (gut) and nervous systems, so it causes a wide range of illnesses. Fox and urban stray dog populations are most at risk and are usually responsible for local outbreaks.

KENNEL COUGH

Also known as infectious tracheobronchitis, *Bordetella bronchiseptica* is not only a major cause of kennel cough but also a common secondary infection on top of another cause. Being a bacterium, it is susceptible to treatment with appropriate antibiotics, but the immunity stimulated by the vaccine is therefore short-lived (six to 12 months).

This vaccine is often in a form to be administered down the nostrils in order to stimulate local immunity at the point of entry, so to speak. Do not be alarmed to see your veterinary surgeon using a needle and syringe to draw up the vaccine, because the needle will be replaced with a special plastic introducer, allowing the vaccine to be gently instilled into each nostril. Dogs generally resent being held more than the actual intra-nasal vaccine, and I have learnt that covering the patient's eyes helps greatly.

Kennel cough is, however, rather a catch-all term for any cough spreading within a dog population – not just in kennels,

Kennel Cough is highly infectious and will spread when dogs live together.

but also between dogs at a training session or breed show, or even mixing in the park. Many of these infections may not be *B. bronchiseptica* but other viruses, for which one can only treat symptomatically. Parainfluenza virus is often included in a vaccine programme, as it is a common viral cause of kennel cough.

Kennel cough can seem alarming. There is a persistent cough accompanied by the production of white frothy spittle, which can last for a matter of weeks; during this time the patient is highly infectious to other dogs. I remember when it

ran through our five Border Collies – there were white patches of froth on the floor wherever you looked! Other features include sneezing, a runny nose, and eyes sore with conjunctivitis. Fortunately, these infections are generally self-limiting, most dogs recovering without any long-lasting problems, but an elderly dog may be knocked sideways by it, akin to the effects of a common cold on a frail, elderly person.

LEPTOSPIROSIS

This disease is caused by *Leptospira interogans*, a spiral-shaped bacterium. There are several natural variants or serovars. Each is characteristically found in one or more particular host animal species, which then acts as a reservoir, intermittently shedding leptospires in the urine. Infection can also be picked up at mating, via bite wounds, across the placenta, or through eating the carcases of infected animals (such as rats).

A serovar will cause actual clinical disease in an individual when two conditions are fulfilled: the individual is not the natural host species, and is also not immune to that particular serovar.

Leptospirosis is a zoonotic disease, known as Weil's disease in humans, with implications for all those in contact with an affected dog. It is also commonly called rat jaundice, reflecting the rat's important role as a carrier. The UK National Rodent Survey 2003 found a wild brown rat population of 60 million, equivalent at the time to one rat per person. Wherever you live in the UK, rats are endemic, which means that there is as much a risk to the Shih Tzu living with a family in a town as the Shih Tzu leading a rural lifestyle.

Signs of illness reflect the organs affected by a particular serovar. In humans, there may be a flu-like illness or a more serious, often life-threatening disorder involving major body organs. The illness in a susceptible dog may be mild, the dog recovering within two to three weeks without treatment but going on to develop long-term liver or kidney disease. In contrast, peracute illness may result in a rapid deterioration and death following an initial malaise and fever. There may also be anorexia, vomiting, diarrhoea, abdominal pain, joint pain, increased thirst and urination rate, jaundice, and ocular changes. Haemorrhage is also a common feature, manifesting as bleeding under the skin, nosebleeds, and the presence of blood in the urine and faeces.

Treatment requires rigorous intravenous fluid therapy to support the kidneys. Being a bacterial infection, it is possible to treat leptospirosis with specific antibiotics, although a prolonged course of several weeks is

The vet will give your Shih Tzu a comprehensive check-up when he goes for his booster vaccination.

needed. Strict hygiene and barrier nursing are required in order to avoid onward transmission of the disease.

Annual vaccination is recommended for leptospirosis because the immunity only lasts for a year, unlike the longer immunity associated with vaccines against viruses. There is, however, little or no cross-protection between Leptospira serovars, so vaccination will result in protection against only those serovars included in the particular vaccine used. Additionally, although vaccination against leptospirosis will prevent active disease if an individual is exposed to a serovar included in the vaccine, it cannot prevent that individual from being infected and becoming a carrier in the long-term.

In the UK, vaccines have classically included *L icterohaemorrhagiae* (rat-adapted serovar) and *L canicola* (dog-specific serovar). The latter is of especial significance to us humans, since disease will not be apparent in an infected dog but leptospires will be shed intermittently.

The situation in America is less clear-cut. Blanket vaccination against leptospirosis is not considered necessary, because it only occurs in certain areas. There has also been a shift in the serovars implicated in clinical

The incidence of Lyme disease is still at a low level in the UK.

disease, reflecting the effectiveness of vaccination and the migration of wildlife reservoirs carrying different serovars from rural areas, so you must be guided by your veterinarian's knowledge of the local situation.

LYME DISEASE
This is a bacterial infection transmitted by hard ticks. It is restricted to those specific areas of the US where ticks are found, such as the north-eastern states, some southern states, California and the upper Mississippi region. It does also occur in the UK, but at a low level, so vaccination is not routinely offered.

Clinical disease is manifested primarily as limping, due to arthritis, but other organs affected include the heart, kidneys and nervous system. It is readily treatable with appropriate

antibiotics, once diagnosed, but the causal bacterium, *Borrelia burgdorferi*, is not cleared from the body totally and will persist. Prevention requires both vaccination and tick control, especially as there are other diseases transmitted by ticks. Ticks carrying *B. burgdorferi* will transmit it to humans as well, but an infected dog cannot pass it to a human.

PARVOVIRUS (CPV)
Canine parvovirus disease first appeared in the late 1970s, when it was feared that the UK's dog population would be decimated by it because of the lack of immunity in the general canine population. While this was a terrifying possibility at the time, fortunately it did not happen.

There are two forms of the virus (CPV-1, CPV-2) affecting domesticated dogs. It is highly

RABIES

This is another zoonotic disease and there are very strict control measures in place. Vaccines were once available in the UK only on an individual basis for dogs being taken abroad. Pets travelling into the UK had to serve six months' compulsory quarantine, so that any pet incubating rabies would be identified before release back into the general population. Under the Pet Travel Scheme (PETS), provided certain criteria are met (check the DEFRA website for up-to-date information), dogs can re-enter the UK without being quarantined.

Dogs to be imported into the US have to show that they were vaccinated against rabies at least 30 days previously; otherwise, they have to serve effective internal quarantine for 30 days from the date of vaccination against rabies, in order to ensure they are not incubating the disease. The exception is dogs entering from countries recognised as being rabies-free, in which case it has to be proved that they lived in that country for at least six months beforehand.

contagious, picked up via the mouth/nose from infected faeces. The incubation period is about five days. CPV-2 causes two types of illness: gastro-enteritis and heart disease in puppies born to unvaccinated dams, both of which often result in death. Infection of puppies under three weeks of age with CPV-1 manifests as diarrhoea, vomiting, difficulty breathing, and fading puppy syndrome. CPV-1 can cause abortion and foetal abnormalities in breeding bitches.

Occurrence is mainly low now, thanks to vaccination, although a recent outbreak in my area did claim the lives of several puppies and dogs. It is also occasionally seen in the elderly unvaccinated dog.

PARASITES

A parasite is defined as an organism deriving benefit on a one-way basis from another, the host. It goes without saying that it is not to the parasite's advantage to harm the host to such an extent that the benefit is lost, especially if it results in the death of the host. This means a dog could harbour parasites, internal and/or external, without there being any signs apparent to the owner. Many canine parasites can, however, transfer to humans with variable consequences, so routine preventative treatment is advised against particular parasites.

Just as with vaccination, risk assessment plays a part – for example, there is no need for

routine heartworm treatment in the UK (at present), but it is vital in the US and in Mediterranean countries.

ROUNDWORM (NEMATODES)
These are the spaghetti-like worms that you may have seen passed in faeces or brought up in vomit. Most of the deworming treatments in use today cause the adults roundworms to disintegrate, thankfully, so that treating puppies in particular is not as unpleasant as it used to be!

Most puppies will have a worm burden, mainly of a particular roundworm species (*Toxocara canis*), which reactivates within the dam's tissues during pregnancy and passes to the foetuses developing in the womb. It is therefore important to treat the dam both during and after pregnancy, as well as the puppies.

Professional advice is to continue worming every one to three months. There are roundworm eggs in the environment and, unless you examine your dog's faeces under a microscope on a very regular basis for the presence of roundworm eggs, you will be unaware of your dog having picked up roundworms, unless he should have such a heavy burden that he passes the adults.

It takes a few weeks from the time that a dog swallows a *Toxocara canis* roundworm egg to himself passing viable eggs (the pre-patent period). These eggs are not immediately infective to other animals, requiring a period of maturation in the environment, which is primarily temperature-dependent and therefore shorter in the summer (as little as two weeks) than in the winter. The eggs can survive in the environment for two years and more.

There are deworming products that are active all the time, which will provide continuous protection when administered as often as directed. Otherwise, treating every month will, in effect, cut in before a dog could theoretically become a source of roundworm eggs to the general population.

It is the risk to human health that is so important: *T. canis* roundworms will migrate within our tissues and cause all manner of problems, not least of which (but fortunately rarely) is blindness. If a dog has roundworms, the eggs also find their way on to his coat where they can be picked up during stroking. Sensible hygiene is therefore important. You should always carefully pick up your dog's faeces and dispose of them appropriately, thereby preventing the maturation of any eggs present in the fresh faeces.

Puppies must be routinely treated for roundworm.

TAPEWORM (CESTODES)

When considering the general dog population, the primary source of the most common tapeworm species will be fleas, which can carry the eggs. Most multi-wormers will be active against these tapeworms. They are not a threat to human health, but it is unpleasant to see the wriggly ricegrain tapeworm segments emerging from your dog's back passage while he is lying in front of the fire, and usually when you have guests for dinner!

A tapeworm of significance to human health is *Echinococcus granulosus*, found in a few parts of the UK, mainly in Wales. Man is an intermediate host for this tapeworm, along with sheep, cattle and pigs. Inadvertent ingestion of eggs passed in the faeces of an infected dog is followed by the development of so-called hydatid cysts in major organs, such as the lungs and liver, necessitating surgical removal. Dogs become infected through eating raw meat containing hydatid cysts. Cooking will kill hydatid cysts, so avoid feeding raw meat and offal in areas of high risk.

There are specific requirements for treatment with praziquantel within 24 to 48 hours of return into the UK under the PETS. This is to prevent the introduction of *Echinococcus multilocularis*, a tapeworm carried by foxes on mainland Europe, which is transmissible to humans, causing serious or even fatal liver disease.

HEARTWORM (DIROFILARIA IMMITIS)

Heartworm infection has been diagnosed in dogs all over the world. There are two prerequisites: the presence of mosquitoes, and a warm, humid climate.

It is essential that all worming treatments are up to date if you plan to travel abroad with your Shih Tzu.

UK's climate, however, could change that.

It is a potentially life-threatening condition, with dogs of all breeds and ages being susceptible without preventative treatment. The larvae can grow to 14 inches within the right side of the heart, causing primarily signs of heart failure and ultimately liver and kidney damage. It can be treated but prevention is a better plan. In the US, regular blood tests for the presence of infection are advised, coupled with appropriate preventative measures, so I would advise liaison with your veterinary surgeon.

For dogs travelling to heartworm-endemic areas of the EU, such as the Mediterranean coast, preventative treatment should be started before leaving the UK and maintained during the visit. Again, this is best arranged with your veterinary surgeon.

FLEAS

There are several species of flea, which are not host-specific. A dog can be carrying cat and human fleas as well as dog fleas, but the same flea treatment will kill and/or control them all. It is also accepted that environmental control is a vital part of a flea control programme. This is because the adult flea is only on the animal for as long as it takes to have a blood meal and to breed; the remainder of the life cycle occurs in the house, car, caravan, shed...

There is a vast array of flea

When a female mosquito bites an infected animal, it acquires *D. immitis* in its circulating form, as microfilariae. A warm environmental temperature is needed for these microfilariae to develop into the infective third-stage larvae (L3) within the mosquitoes, the so-called intermediate host. L3 larvae are then transmitted by the mosquito when it next bites a dog. Therefore, while heartworm infection is found in all parts of the United States, it is at differing levels. An occurrence in Alaska, for example, is probably a reflection of a visiting dog having previously picked up the infection elsewhere.

Heartworm infection is not currently a problem in the UK, except for those dogs contracting it while abroad without suitable preventative treatment. Global warming and its effect on the

control products available, with various routes of administration: collar, powder, spray, 'spot-on', or oral. Flea control needs to be applied to all pets in the house, regardless of whether they leave the house, since fleas can be introduced into the home by other pets and their human owners. Discuss your specific flea control needs with your veterinary surgeon.

MITES

There are five types of mite which can affect dogs:

i. Demodex canis: This mite is a normal inhabitant of canine hair follicles, passed from the bitch to her pups as they suckle. The development of actual skin disease or demodicosis depends on the individual. It is seen frequently around the time of puberty and after a bitch's first season, associated with hormonal changes. There may, however, be an inherited weakness in an individual's immune system enabling multiplication of the mite. The localised form consists of areas of fur loss without itchiness, generally around the face and on the forelimbs, and 90 per cent will recover without treatment.

The other 10 per cent develop the juvenile-onset generalised form, of which half will recover spontaneously. The other half may be depressed, go off their food, and show signs of itchiness due to secondary bacterial skin infections. Treatment is often prolonged over several months and consists of regular bathing with a specific miticidal shampoo, often clipping away fur to improve access to the skin, together with a suitable antibiotic by mouth. There is also now a licensed 'spot-on' preparation available. Progress is monitored by examination of deep skin scrapings for the presence of the mite; the initial diagnosis is based upon abnormally high numbers of the mite, often with live individuals being seen.

There is a third group of individuals developing demodicosis for the first time in middle-age (more than about four years of age), and as the generalised form. This is often reflecting underlying immunosuppression by an internal disease process, such as neoplasia, or treatment with corticosteroids, for example, so it is important to identify any predisposing cause and correct it where possible, as well as specifically treating as above.

(ii) Sarcoptes scabei: This mite characteristically causes an intense pruritus or itchiness in the affected dog, causing the dog to incessantly scratch and bite at himself, leading to marked fur

Remember to give your Shih Tzu a thorough check after returning from walks.

loss and skin trauma. Initially starting on the elbows, ear flaps and hocks, without treatment the skin on the rest of the body can become involved, with thickening and pigmentation of the skin. Secondary bacterial infections are common.

Unlike *Demodex*, this mite lives at the skin surface, and it can be hard to find in skin scrapings. It is therefore not unusual to treat a patient for sarcoptic mange (scabies) based on the appearance of the problem even with negative skin scraping findings, and especially if there is a history of contact with foxes, which are a frequent source of the scabies mite. It will spread between dogs and can therefore also be found in situations where large numbers of dogs from different backgrounds are mixing together. It should be noted that it will cause itchiness in humans, although the mite cannot complete its life cycle on us, so treating all affected dogs should be sufficient.

Fortunately, there is now a highly effective 'spot-on' treatment for Sarcoptes scabei.

(iii) Cheyletiella yasguri: This is the fur mite most commonly found on dogs. It is often called 'walking dandruff' because it can be possible to see collections of the small white mite moving about over the skin surface. There is excessive scale and dandruff formation, and mild itchiness. It is important as a zoonosis, being transmissible to humans where it causes a pruritic rash.

Diagnosis is by microscopic examination of skin scrapings, coat combings and sticky tape impressions from the skin and fur. Treatment is with an appropriate insecticide, as advised by your veterinary surgeon.

(iv) Otodectes cynotis: A highly transmissible otitis externa (outer ear infection) results from the presence in the outer ear canal of this ear mite, characterised by exuberant production of dark ear wax. The patient will frequently shake his head and rub at the ear(s) affected. The mites can also spread to the skin adjacent to the opening of the external ear canal, and may transfer elsewhere, such as to the paws.

When using an otoscope to examine the outer ear canal, the heat from the light source will often cause any ear mites present to start moving around. I often offer owners the chance to have a look because it really is quite an extraordinary sight! It is also possible to identify the mite from ear wax smeared onto a slide and examined under a microscope.

Cats are a common source of ear mites. It is not unusual to find ear mites during the routine examination of puppies and kittens. Treatment options include specific ear drops acting against both the mite and any secondary infections present in the auditory canal, and certain 'spot-on' formulations. It is vital to treat all dogs and cats in the household to prevent re-cycling of the mite between individuals.

(v) The free-living mite (Neo-Trombicula autumnalis) or harvest mite: This mite can cause an intense local irritation

TICKS

Ticks have become an increasing problem in recent years throughout Britain. Their physical presence causes irritation, but it is their potential to spread disease that causes concern. A tick will transmit any infection previously contracted while feeding on an animal: for example *Borrelia burgdorferi*, the causal agent of Lyme disease.

The life cycle of the tick is curious: each life stage takes a year to develop and move on to the next. Long grass is a major habitat. The vibration of animals moving through the grass will stimulate the larva, nymph or adult to climb up a blade of grass and wave its legs in the air as it 'quests' for a host on to which to latch for its next blood meal. Humans are as likely to be hosts, so ramblers and orienteers are advised to cover their legs when going through rough long grass.

Removing a tick is simple – provided your dog will stay still. The important rule is to twist gently so that the tick is persuaded to let go with its mouthparts. Grasp the body of the tick as near to your dog's skin as possible, either between thumb and fingers or with a specific tick-removing instrument, and then rotate in one direction until the tick comes away. I keep a plastic tick hook in my wallet at all times.

on the skin. Its larvae are picked up from undergrowth, so they are characteristically found as a bright orange patch on the web of skin between the digits of the paws. It feeds on skin cells before dropping off to complete its life cycle in the environment.

Its name is a little misleading because it is not restricted to the autumn nor to harvest-time; I find it on the ear flaps of cats from late June onwards, depending on the prevailing weather. It will also bite humans. Treatment depends on identifying and avoiding hotspots for picking up harvest mite, if possible. Checking the skin (especially the paws) after exercise, and mechanically removing any mites found will reduce the chances of irritation, which can be treated symptomatically. Insecticides can also be applied – be guided by your veterinary surgeon.

A-Z OF COMMON AILMENTS

ANAL SACS (IMPACTED)

The anal sacs lie on either side of the anus at approximately four and eight o'clock, if compared with the face of a clock. They fill with a particularly pungent fluid, which is emptied on to the faeces as they move past the sacs to exit from the anus. Theories abound as to why these sacs should become impacted periodically and seemingly more so in some dogs than others.

The irritation of impacted anal sacs is often seen as 'scooting', when the backside is dragged along the ground. Some dogs will also gnaw at their back feet or over the rump.

Increasing the fibre content of the diet helps some dogs; in others, there is underlying skin disease. It may be a one-off occurrence for no apparent reason. Sometimes an infection can become established, requiring antibiotic therapy, which may need to be coupled with flushing out the infected sac under sedation or general anaesthesia. More rarely, a dog will present with an apparently acute-onset anal sac abscess, which is incredibly painful.

DIARRHOEA

Cause and treatment much as Gastritis (see below).

EAR INFECTIONS

The dog has a long external ear canal, initially vertical then horizontal, leading to the eardrum, which protects the middle ear. If your Shih Tzu is shaking his head, then his ears will need to be inspected with an

The ears must be kept clean and excess hair should be removed from the inside to reduce the risk of infection.

auroscope by a veterinary surgeon in order to identify any cause, and to ensure the eardrum is intact. A sample may be taken from the canal to be examined under the microscope and cultured, to identify causal agents before prescribing appropriate eardrops containing antibiotic, antifungal agent and/or steroid. Predisposing causes of otitis externa or infection in the external ear canal include:

- Presence of a foreign body, such as a grass awn
- Ear mites, which are intensely irritating to the dog and stimulate the production of brown wax, predisposing to infection
- Previous infections, causing the canal's lining to thicken, narrowing the canal and reducing ventilation
- water trapped in the external ear canal can lead to infection – the Shih Tzu rarely likes swimming, but care should be taken when bathing him..

FOREIGN BODIES

Internal: Items swallowed in haste without checking whether they will be digested can cause problems if they lodge in the stomach or obstruct the intestines, necessitating surgical removal. Acute vomiting is the main sign. Common objects I have seen removed include stones from the garden, peach stones, babies' dummies, golf balls and, once, a lady's bra... It is possible to diagnose a dog with an intestinal obstruction across a waiting room from a

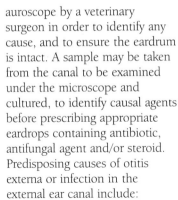

particularly 'tucked-up' stance and pained facial expression. These patients bounce back from surgery dramatically. A previously docile and compliant obstructed patient will return for a post-operative check-up and literally bounce into the consulting room.

External: Grass awns are adept at finding their way into orifices such as a nostril, down an ear, and into the soft skin between two digits (toes), whence they start a one-way journey due to the direction of their whiskers. In particular, I remember a grass awn that migrated from a hindpaw, causing abscesses along the way but not yielding itself up until it erupted through the skin in the groin!

GASTRITIS

This is usually a simple stomach upset, most commonly in response to dietary indiscretion. Scavenging constitutes a change in the diet as much as an abrupt switch in the food being fed by the owner. There are also some specific infections causing more severe gastritis/enteritis, which will require treatment from a veterinary surgeon (see also Canine Parvovirus under 'Vaccination' earlier).

Generally, a day without food, followed by a few days of small, frequent meals of a bland diet (such as cooked chicken or fish), or an appropriate prescription diet, should allow the stomach to settle. It is vital to ensure the patient is drinking and retaining sufficient water to cover losses

Stiffness after exercise can be a problem with older dogs.

resulting from the stomach upset in addition to the normal losses to be expected when healthy. Oral rehydration fluid may not be very appetising for the patient, in which case cooled boiled water should be offered. Fluids should initially be offered in small but frequent amounts to avoid over-drinking, which can result in further vomiting and thereby dehydration and electrolyte imbalances. It is also important to wean the patient back on to routine food gradually or else another bout of gastritis may occur.

JOINT PROBLEMS

It is not unusual for older Shih Tzus to be stiff after exercise, particularly in cold weather. This is not really surprising, given that they are such busy dogs when young. This is such a game breed that a nine- or ten-year-old Shih Tzu will not readily forego an extra walk or take kindly to turning for home earlier than usual.

Your veterinary surgeon will be able to advise you on ways of helping your Shih Tzu cope with joint stiffness, not least of which will be to ensure that he is not overweight. Arthritic joints do not need to be burdened with extra bodyweight!

LUMPS & BUMPS

Regularly handling and stroking your dog will enable the early detection of lumps and bumps. These may be due a number of causes, including infection (abscess), bruising, multiplication of particular cells from within the body, or even an external parasite (tick). If you are worried about any lump you find, have it checked by a veterinary surgeon.

OBESITY

Being overweight does predispose to many other problems, such as diabetes mellitus, heart disease and joint problems. It is so easily prevented by simply acting as your Shih Tzu's conscience. Ignore pleading eyes and feed according to your dog's waistline. The body condition is what matters qualitatively, alongside monitoring that individual's bodyweight as a quantitative measure. The Shih Tzu should, in my opinion as a health professional, have at least a suggestion of a waist and it should be possible to feel the ribs beneath only a slight layer of fat.

Do remember that, to human eyes, your Shih Tzu's food intake will seem very small. Everything is proportionate, however, and even the smallest tidbit will be a significant addition to the diet of your dog. You must be ever vigilant if your Shih Tzu is to retain a waistline.

Neutering does not automatically mean that your Shih Tzu will be overweight. Having an ovario-hysterectomy does slow down the body's rate of working, castration to a lesser extent, but it therefore means that your dog needs less food. I recommend cutting back a little on the amount of food fed a few weeks before neutering to accustom your Shih Tzu to less food. If she looks a little underweight on the morning of the operation, it will help the

It is the owner's responsibility to safeguard dental health.

veterinary surgeon as well as giving her a little leeway weight-wise afterwards. It is always harder to lose weight after neutering than before, because of this slowing in the body's inherent metabolic rate.

TEETH

Eating food starts with the canine teeth gripping and killing prey in the wild, incisor teeth biting off pieces of food and the molar teeth chewing it. To be able to eat is vital for life, yet the actual health of the teeth is often overlooked: unhealthy teeth can predispose to disease, and not just by reducing the ability to eat. The presence of infection within the mouth can lead to bacteria entering the bloodstream and then filtering out at major organs, with the potential for serious consequences. That is not to

forget that simply having dental pain can affect a dog's wellbeing, as anyone who has had toothache will confirm.

Veterinary dentistry has made huge leaps in recent years, so that it no longer consists of extraction as the treatment of necessity. Good dental health lies in the hands of the owner, starting from the moment the dog comes into your care. Just as we have taken on responsibility for feeding, so we have acquired the task of maintaining good dental and oral hygiene. In an ideal world, we should brush our dogs' teeth as regularly as our own, but the Shih Tzu puppy who finds having his teeth brushed is a huge game and excuse to roll over and over on the ground requires loads of patience, twice a day.

There are alternative strategies, ranging from dental chewsticks to specially formulated foods, but the main thing is to be aware of your dog's mouth. At least train your puppy to permit full examination of his teeth. This will not only ensure you are checking in his mouth regularly but will also make your veterinary surgeon's job easier when there is a real need for your dog to 'open wide!'

INHERITED DISORDERS

Any individual, dog or human, may have an inherited disorder by virtue of the genes acquired from the parents. This is significant not only for the health of that individual but also because of the potential for transmitting the disorder on to that individual's offspring and to subsequent generations, depending on the mode of inheritance.

There are control schemes in place for some inherited disorders. In the US, for example, the Canine Eye Registration Foundation (CERF) was set up by dog breeders concerned about heritable eye disease, and provides a database of dogs who have been examined by diplomates of the American College of Veterinary Ophthalmologists.

The Shih Tzu is a breed where very few inherited conditions have been confirmed. The breed has a brachycephalic skull resulting in a foreshortened nose and shallow orbits (the bony eye sockets). This predisposes to the eyeballs being more prominent and a reduced ability to close the eyelids over them. This in turn predisposes to Exposure Keratitis or inflammation of the cornea which, at its most extreme, can lead to ulceration and rupture. Proptosis is another risk, whereby the eyeball is displaced out of the socket and the eyelids close behind the eyeball, compromising the blood supply to the retina. Blindness can result rapidly so urgent veterinary attention must be sought.

To date, only a few conditions have been confirmed in the Shih Tzu as being hereditary. In alphabetical order, these include:

CATARACTS (HEREDITARY OR JUVENILE)

These are a concern in the US, affecting one or both eyes with partial or complete opacification of the lens(es). The effect on vision will therefore vary on an individual basis, with complete blindness when there is a complete cataract in both eyes. CERF recommends annual eye testing.

ENTROPION

This is an inrolling of the eyelids. There are degrees of entropion, ranging from a slight inrolling to the more serious case, requiring surgical correction because of the pain and damage to the surface of the eyeball.

KERATOCONJUNCTIVITIS SICCA (KCS, DRY EYE)

Each eye is lubricated by tears produced by two tear glands, one within the eye socket and another smaller one associated with the third eyelid. There appears to be a breed predisposition for KCS which results when there is inadequate tear production by the glands (hence 'dry eye'), and is usually bilateral, affecting the tear glands in both eyes. It is characterised by a sore red appearance to the eye with a thick ocular discharge and, ultimately,

It is essential that breeding stock has all the relevant health checks to help eliminate the incidence of inherited disease.

clouding of the cornea and loss of vision. The cause is generally unknown or inherited but, rarely, dry eye may result from trauma, infection, hypothyroidism or an adverse reaction to a drug.

Diagnosis is made with a Schirmer tear strip which assesses the tear production in each eye. Surgical transposition of the parotid salivary duct was the favoured treatment, but medical therapy is now more often the therapy of choice, aimed at stimulating the under-active tear glands.

PROGRESSIVE RETINAL ATROPHY (PRA)

This is of concern in the US. Degeneration of the retina first manifests as night blindness in the young animal. It is a progressive disorder, culminating in total blindness.

RENAL DYSPLASIA, JUVENILE (JRD)

Affected individuals develop the signs of kidney failure from a few months of age. There may also be concurrent Renal Glucosuria as well: the presence of glucose in the urine with a normal blood glucose level (unlike the situation in diabetes mellitus where there is hyperglycaemia, or raised blood glucose). A gene mutation underlying JRD, which is inherited as dominant with incomplete penetrance, has been identified in the US; DNA testing for it can now be performed on cheek swab samples.

UROLITHIASIS

Urolithiasis is the presence of stones or excessive amounts of crystals within the urinary tract, most commonly in the bladder. They irritate the lining of the urinary tract, resulting in pain and blood in the urine. They may predispose to a secondary bacterial infection. In some instances, they may actually partially or totally block the outflow of urine which requires emergency treatment.

There are different biochemical types of uroliths. Surveys of Shih Tzus have found a higher than expected incidence of various types of urolithiasis.

COMPLEMENTARY THERAPIES

Just as for human health, I do believe that there is a place for alternative therapies alongside and complementing orthodox treatment under the supervision of a veterinary surgeon. That is why 'complementary therapies' is a better name.

Because animals do not have a choice, there are measures in place to safeguard their wellbeing and welfare. All manipulative treatment must be under the direction of a veterinary surgeon who has examined the patient and diagnosed the condition that he or she feels needs that form of treatment. This covers physiotherapy, chiropractic, osteopathy and swimming therapy. For example, dogs with arthritis who cannot exercise as freely as they were accustomed will enjoy the sensation of controlled non-weight-bearing exercise in water, and will benefit with improved muscling and overall fitness.

All other complementary therapies such as acupuncture, homoeopathy and aromatherapy,

Increasingly owners are becoming aware of the benefit of complementary therapies to promote health and wellbeing.

With good care and management, your Shih Tzu should live a long, happy and healthy life.

can only be carried out by veterinary surgeons who have been trained in that particular field. Acupuncture is mainly used in dogs for pain relief, often to good effect. The needles look more alarming to the owner, but they are very fine and are well tolerated by most canine patients. Speaking personally, superficial needling is not unpleasant and does help with pain relief. Homoeopathy has had a mixed press in recent years. It is based on the concept of treating like with like. Additionally, a homoeopathic remedy is said to become more powerful the more it is diluted.

SUMMARY

As the owner of a Shih Tzu, you are responsible for his care and health. Not only must you make decisions on his behalf, you are also responsible for establishing a lifestyle for him that will ensure he leads a long and happy life. Diet plays as important a part in this, as does exercise.

For the domestic dog, it is only in recent years that the need has been recognised for changing the diet to suit the dog as he grows, matures and then enters his twilight years. So-called life-stage diets try to match the nutritional needs of the dog as he progresses through life.

An adult dog food will suit the Shih Tzu living a standard family life. There are also foods for those Shih Tzus tactfully termed as obese-prone, such as those who have been neutered or are less active than others, or simply like their food. Do remember, though, that ultimately you are in control of your Shih Tzu's diet, unless he is able to profit from scavenging!

On the other hand, prescription diets are of necessity fed under the supervision of a veterinary surgeon because each is formulated to meet the very specific needs of a particular health condition. Should a prescription diet be fed to a healthy dog, or to a dog with a different illness, there could be adverse effects.

It is important to remember that your Shih Tzu has no choice. As his owner, you are responsible for any decision made, so it must be as informed a decision as possible. Always speak to your veterinary surgeon if you have any worries about your Shih Tzu. He is not just a dog: from the moment you brought him home, he became a member of the family.

THE CONTRIBUTORS

THE EDITOR:
JULIETTE CUNLIFFE
(MODHISH)

Juliette Cunliffe has owned show dogs for 34 years and has judged Shih Tzu at Championship level in the UK since 1998. She has judged the breed many times abroad, in Belgium, Eire, Holland, Latvia, Luxembourg, Russia, Sweden and Slovenia, sometimes more than once.

Having had considerable success as an exhibitor and breeder, Juliette now lives in the Himalaya but still thoroughly enjoys judging. She still shares her home with four much-loved dogs, three of which are show dogs who travelled over with her from the UK.

Apart from being a regular columnist in the canine press, Juliette is highly regarded throughout the world as a canine author. Several of her books have also been printed in German and Spanish, but it came as some surprise to her when a Russian dog book dropped through her letter-box one day – when she had deciphered the writing, it turned out to be her very first Shih Tzu book, re-printed in Russia!

See Chapter One: Getting to Know Shih Tzu; Chapter Two: The First Shih Tzu; Chapter Three: A Shih Tzu for Your Lifestyle; Chapter Four: The New Arrival; Chapter Seven: The Perfect Shih Tzu.

CAROL STOBBS (SONOMA)

Shih Tzu have been a part of Carol's life since 1987, although she and her husband Rob didn't start showing until 1994 (with Berylendan's Archimedes of Sonoma – 'Archie'.)

Carol and Rob pride themselves on breeding dogs with sound temperament, producing dogs with the typical Shih Tzu character. Health is also very high on their list of priorities.

Carol is the Assistant Secretary of the Manchu Shih Tzu Society and judges at Open Show level.
See Chapter Five: The Best of Care..

JULIA BARNES

Julia has owned and trained a number of different dog breeds, and has also worked as a puppy socialiser for Dogs for the Disabled. A former journalist, she has written many books, including several on dog training and behaviour. Julia is indebted to Margaret Stangeland for her specialist knowledge about training Shih Tzu.
See Chapter Six: Training and Socialisation.

MARGARET STANGELAND (WEATSOM)

Margaret has lived with dogs all her life; she first started showing Yorkshire Terriers, and then Maltese, but when she saw her first Shih Tzu she was completely won over and knew that that was the breed for her.
. Margaret has now been in the breed for over 30 years, and has been very successful making up 19 Champions to date under her Weatsom affix, including one international Champion.

She has judged Shih Tzu judged at CC level eight times, and also travelled abroad to judge the breed in Holland and Sweden.

She says: "The Shih Tzu is a wonderful, funny, clever, loyal friend for young and old alike – and I could never be without one".
See Chapter Six: Training and Socialisation.

ALISON LOGAN MA VetMB MRCVS

Alison qualified as a veterinary surgeon from Cambridge University in 1989, having been brought up surrounded by all manner of animals and birds in the north Essex countryside. She has been in practice in her home town ever since, living with her husband, two children and Labrador Retriever Pippin.

She contributes on a regular basis to *Veterinary Times, Veterinary Nurse Times, Dogs Today, Cat World* and *Pet Patter,* the PetPlan newsletter. In 1995, Alison won the Univet Literary Award with an article on Cushing's Disease, and she won it again (as the Vetoquinol Literary Award) in 2002, writing about common conditions in the Shar-Pei.
See Chapter Eight: Happy and Healthy.

USEFUL ADDRESSES

KENNEL & BREED CLUBS

UK

The Kennel Club
1 Clarges Street, London, W1J 8AB
Tel: 0870 606 6750
Fax: 0207 518 1058
Web: www.the-kennel-club.org.uk

To obtain up-to-date contact information for the following breed clubs, please contact the Kennel Club:
• Manchu Shih Tzu Society
• Northern Counties Shih Tzu Club
• Shih Tzu Club
• Shih Tzu Club of Scotland
• Shih Tzu Club of South Wales and
  Western Counties.

USA

American Kennel Club (AKC)
5580 Centerview Drive,
Raleigh, NC 27606, USA.
Tel: 919 233 9767
Fax: 919 233 3627
Email: info@akc.org
Web: www.akc.org

United Kennel Club (UKC)
100 E Kilgore Rd, Kalamazoo,
MI 49002-5584, USA.
Tel: 269 343 9020
Fax: 269 343 7037
Web:www.ukcdogs.com/

American Shih Tzu Club
5252 Shafter Avenue,
Oakland, CA 94618.
Web:

For contact details of regional clubs, please contact the American Shih Tzu Club.

AUSTRALIA
Australian National Kennel Council (ANKC)
The Australian National Kennel Council is the administrative body for pure breed canine affairs in Australia. It does not, however, deal directly with dog exhibitors, breeders or judges. For information pertaining to breeders, clubs or shows, please contact the relevant State or Territory Controlling Body.

Dogs Australian Capital Teritory
PO Box 815, Dickson ACT 2602
Tel: (02) 6241 4404
Fax: (02) 6241 1129
Email: administrator@dogsact.org.au
Web: www.dogsact.org.au

Dogs New South Wales
PO Box 632, St Marys, NSW 1790
Tel: (02) 9834 3022 or 1300 728 022
(NSW Only)
Fax: (02) 9834 3872
Email: info@dogsnsw.org.au
Web: www.dogsnsw.org.au

Dogs Northern Territory
PO Box 37521, Winnellie NT 0821
Tel: (08) 8984 3570
Fax: (08) 8984 3409
Email: admin@dogsnt.com.au
Web: www.dogsnt.com.au

Dogs Queensland
PO Box 495, Fortitude Valley Qld 4006
Tel: (07) 3252 2661
Fax: (07) 3252 3864
Email: info@dogsqueensland.org.au
Web: www.dogsqueensland.org.au

Dogs South Australia
PO Box 844
Prospect East SA 5082
Tel: (08) 8349 4797
Fax: (08) 8262 5751
Email: info@dogssa.com.au
Web: www.dogssa.com.au

Tasmanian Canine Association Inc
The Rothman Building
PO Box 116
Glenorchy Tas 7010
Tel: (03) 6272 9443
Fax: (03) 6273 0844
Email: tca@iprimus.com.au
Web: www.tasdogs.com

Dogs Victoria
Locked Bag K9
Cranbourne VIC 3977
Tel: (03)9788 2500
Fax: (03) 9788 2599
Email: office@dogsvictoria.org.au
Web: www.dogsvictoria.org.au

Dogs Western Australia
PO Box 1404
Canning Vale WA 6970
Tel: (08) 9455 1188
Fax: (08) 9455 1190
Email: k9@dogswest.com
Web: www.dogswest.com

INTERNATIONAL
Fédération Cynologique Internationalé (FCI)/World Canine Organisation
Place Albert 1er, 13, B-6530 Thuin,
Belgium.
Tel: +32 71 59.12.38
Fax: +32 71 59.22.29
Web: www.fci.be/

TRAINING AND BEHAVIOUR

UK
Association of Pet Dog Trainers
PO Box 17, Kempsford, GL7 4WZ
Telephone: 01285 810811
Email: APDToffice@aol.com
Web: http://www.apdt.co.uk

Association of Pet Behaviour Counsellors
PO BOX 46, Worcester, WR8 9YS
Telephone: 01386 751151
Fax: 01386 750743
Email: info@apbc.org.uk
Web: http://www.apbc.org.uk/

USA
Association of Pet Dog Trainers
101 North Main Street, Suite 610
Greenville, SC 29601, USA.
Tel: 1 800 738 3647
Email: information@apdt.com
Web: www.apdt.com/

American College of Veterinary Behaviorists
College of Veterinary Medicine, 4474 Tamu,
Texas A&M University
College Station, Texas 77843-4474
Web: http://dacvb.org/

American Veterinary Society of Animal Behavior
Web: www.avsabonline.org/

AUSTRALIA

APDT Australia Inc
PO Box 3122, Bankstown Square, NSW 2200, Australia.
Email: secretary@apdt.com.au
Web: www.apdt.com.au

Canine Behaviour
For details of regional behvaiourists, contact the relevant State or Territory Controlling Body.

ACTIVITIES

UK
Agility Club
http://www.agilityclub.co.uk/

British Flyball Association
PO Box 990, Doncaster, DN1 9FY
Telephone: 01628 829623
Email: secretary@flyball.org.uk
Web: http://www.flyball.org.uk/

USA

North American Dog Agility Council
P.O. Box 1206, Colbert,
OK 74733, USA.
Web: www.nadac.com/

North American Flyball Association, Inc.
1333 West Devon Avenue, #512
Chicago, IL 60660
Tel/Fax: 800 318 6312
Email: flyball@flyball.org
Web: www.flyball.org/

AUSTRALIA

Agility Dog Association of Australia
ADAA Secretary, PO Box 2212,
Gailes, QLD 4300, Australia.
Tel: 0423 138 914
Email: admin@adaa.com.au
Web: www.adaa.com.au/

**NADAC Australia (North American Dog
Agility Council - Australian Division)**
12 Wellman Street, Box Hill South, Victoria
3128, Australia.
Email: shirlene@nadacaustralia.com
Web: www.nadacaustralia.com/

Australian Flyball Association
PO Box 4179, Pitt Town, NSW 2756
Tel: 0407 337 939
Email: info@flyball.org.au
Web: www.flyball.org.au/

INTERNATIONAL

World Canine Freestyle Organisation
P.O. Box 350122, Brooklyn, NY 11235-
2525, USA
Tel: (718) 332-8336
Fax: (718) 646-2686
Email: wcfodogs@aol.com
Web: www.worldcaninefreestyle.org

HEALTH

UK

Alternative Veterinary Medicine Centre
Chinham House, Stanford in the Vale,
Oxfordshire, SN7 8NQ
Tel: 01367 710324
Fax: 01367 718243
Web: www.alternativevet.org/

**British Small Animal Veterinary
Association**
Woodrow House, 1 Telford Way,
Waterwells Business Park, Quedgeley,
Gloucestershire, GL2 2AB
Tel: 01452 726700
Fax: 01452 726701
Email: customerservices@bsava.com
Web: http://www.bsava.com/

Royal College of Veterinary Surgeons
Belgravia House, 62-64 Horseferry Road,
London, SW1P 2AF
Tel: 0207 222 2001

Fax: 0207 222 2004
Email: admin@rcvs.org.uk
Web: www.rcvs.org.uk

USA

**American Holistic Veterinary Medical
Association**
2218 Old Emmorton Road
Bel Air, MD 21015
Tel: 410 569 0795
Fax 410 569 2346
Email: office@ahvma.org
Web: www.ahvma.org/

American Veterinary Medical Association
1931 North Meacham Road, Suite 100,
Schaumburg, IL 60173-4360, USA.
Tel: 800 248 2862
Fax: 847 925 1329
Web: www.avma.org

American College of Veterinary Surgeons
19785 Crystal Rock Dr, Suite 305
Germantown, MD 20874, USA.
Tel: 301 916 0200
Toll Free: 877 217 2287
Fax: 301 916 2287
Email: acvs@acvs.org
Web: www.acvs.org/

AUSTRALIA

Australian Holistic Vets
Web: www.ahv.com.au/

**Australian Small Animal Veterinary
Association**
40/6 Herbert Street, St Leonards, NSW
2065, Australia.
Tel: 02 9431 5090
Fax: 02 9437 9068
Email: asava@ava.com.au
Web: www.asava.com.au

Australian Veterinary Association
Unit 40, 6 Herbert Street, St Leonards,
NSW 2065, Australia.
Tel: 02 9431 5000
Fax: 02 9437 9068
Web: www.ava.com.au

Australian College Veterinary Scientists
Building 3, Garden City Office Park,
2404 Logan Road, Eight Mile Plains,
Queensland 4113, Australia.
Tel: 07 3423 2016
Fax: 07 3423 2977
Email: admin@acvs.org.au
Web: http://acvsc.org.au

ASSISTANCE DOGS

Canine Partners
Mill Lane, Heyshott, Midhurst,
, GU29 0ED
Tel: 08456 580480
Fax: 08456 580481
Web: www.caninepartners.co.uk

Dogs for the Disabled
The Frances Hay Centre, Blacklocks Hill,
Banbury, Oxon, OX17 2BS
Tel: 01295 252600
Web: www.dogsforthedisabled.org

Guide Dogs for the Blind Association
Burghfield Common, Reading, RG7 3YG
Tel: 01189 835555
Fax: 01189 835433
Web: www.guidedogs.org.uk/

Hearing Dogs for Deaf People
The Grange, Wycombe Road, Saunderton,
Princes Risborough, Bucks, HP27 9NS
Tel: 01844 348100
Fax: 01844 348101
Web: www.hearingdogs.org.uk

Pets as Therapy
3a Grange Farm Cottages, Wycombe Road,
Saunderton, Princes Risborough,
Bucks, HP27 9NS
Tel: 01845 345445
Fax: 01845 550236
Web: http://www.petsastherapy.org/

Support Dogs
21 Jessops Riverside, Brightside Lane,
Sheffield, S9 2RX
Tel: 01142 617800
Fax: 01142 617555
Email: supportdogs@btconnect.com
Web: www.support-dogs.org.uk

USA

Therapy Dogs International
88 Bartley Road, Flanders, NJ 07836,.
Tel: 973 252 9800
Fax: 973 252 7171
Email: tdi@gti.net
Web: www.tdi-dog.o

Therapy Dogs Inc.
P.O. Box 20227, Cheyenne, WY 82003.
Tel: 307 432 0272.
Fax: 307-638-2079
Web: www.therapydogs.com

Delta Society - Pet Partners
875 124th Ave NE, Suite 101 • Bellevue,
WA 98005 USA.
Email: info@DeltaSociety.org
Web: www.deltasociety.org

Comfort Caring Canines
8135 Lare Street, Philadelphia, PA 19128.
Email: ccc@comfortcaringcanines.org
Web: www.comfortcaringcanines.org/

AUSTRALIA

AWARE Dogs Australia, Inc
PO Box 883, Kuranda, Queensland, 488,
Australia.
Tel: 07 4093 8152
Web: www.awaredogs.org.au/

Delta Society — Therapy Dogs
Web: www.deltasociety.com.au